BASICS
INTERIOR DESIGN

retail design

Second edition

BLOOMSBURY VISUAL ARTS
LONDON · NEW YORK · OXFORD · NEW DELHI · SYDNEY

BLOOMSBURY VISUAL ARTS
Bloomsbury Publishing Plc
50 Bedford Square, London, WC1B 3DP, UK
1385 Broadway, New York, NY 10018

BLOOMSBURY, BLOOMSBURY VISUAL ARTS and the Diana logo
are trademarks of Bloomsbury Publishing Plc

First published in Great Britain 2010
This edition published 2020

A catalogue record for this book is available from the British Library.

Library of Congress Cataloging-in-Publication Data
Names: Mesher, Lynne, author. | Anderson, Stephen, 1966- author.
Title: Retail design / Lynne Mesher and Stephen Anderson.
Description: [Second edition]. | New York : Bloomsbury Visual Arts, [2019] |
Includes bibliographical references and index.
Identifiers: LCCN 2018019431 | ISBN 9781474289252 (pbk. : alk. paper) | ISBN
9781350031364 (epub)
Subjects: LCSH: Store decoration.
Classification: LCC NK2195.S89 M46 2019 | DDC 745.4—dc23 LC record
available at https://lccn.loc.gov/2018019431

ISBN: PB: 978-1-4742-8925-2
       ePDF: 978-1-4742-9429-4
       eBook: 978-1-3500-3136-4

Series: Basics Interior Design

Typeset by Lachina Creative, Inc.
Printed and bound in India

To find out more about our authors and books visit
www.bloomsbury.com and sign up for our newsletters.

Figure 0.1 gentSac
Flagship, Sydney Designer:
Landini Associates, 2015

The aim of this book is to examine the processes and strategies of designing space for retail activities.

Retail is a fast-moving industry which is constantly evolving to satisfy a number of ever-changing factors and situations which may be driven by technology, logistics or changing customer expectations. This book aims to provide a clear explanation of the main themes with a solid grounding of retail activities and strategies which will continue to change and develop in the future.

Shopping is an activity that is part of our everyday lives. Whether we are shopping to feed ourselves, clothe ourselves or simply out of enjoyment, the places we choose to shop say something about our lifestyle, culture and interests. We create a relationship with the retail environment we feel comfortable with and reject spaces that do not match our expectations.

The design of shops is an ever-changing cycle, following fashion trends and consumer aspirations. In recent years the shopping experience has been transformed by the increased use of online channels which means the retail environment has to work harder to attract and maintain customer interest.

Figure 0.2 **The Shop at Bluebird, London Designer: Dalziel & Pow, 2018** Located in a 19th century coach house this store curates an eclectic mix of fashion, art, beauty and homewares over three levels. The integration of original elements, found pieces and lush plants provides a sense of ever changing wonder. The main atrium space is enlivened by a bespoke icosahedron installation of 20 mirrored faces that reflect and distort the surroundings. The main staircase also has a reflective underside, as if floating above the greenery.

In response to this, retail spaces are at the forefront of contemporary interior design because they are updated regularly to stay competitive and appealing. Some of the most innovative and interactive interiors can be seen in the retail sector.

Designing retail interiors is a complex process starting with the analysis of the brand and integrating a wide range of product types and experiences into a new or existing space. The aim of the designer is to entice, excite and enthral the consumer by creating an experience to which they can relate.

Retail has become an international business and we now find ourselves shopping for the same brands in similar environments across countries and continents. In contrast to this we seek out engaging experiences unique to a particular brand or location. This has been recognized by analysing and referencing a wide range of international projects both through text and images; detailed case studies are also employed to provide depth and insight.

This book thoroughly guides you through each step of the retail design process, providing strategies that can produce a successful retail space and a design that is appropriate for the brand, product, consumer and retailer. This will be seen through images and drawings from practice, as well as examples of best practice. This new edition extends this to provide a variety of end-of-chapter exercises which have been developed through experience to provide meaningful learning opportunities which readers can use to increase their understanding and knowledge.

The behaviour and profile of the shopper has changed markedly over the past few years and particularly the relationship between the customer and the retailer. This has been driven by a number of factors, not least the availability of products, outlets and channels, as well as demographic and behavioural shifts. This has created a shift from the era of 'the customer is always right' to 'the customer always has a choice'.

THIS CHAPTER will examine some key aspects of the behaviour and psychology of both retailers and consumers and how the two interact with each other for both commercial advantage and engaging experiences. This will help set the scene and context for the practice of retail design and explore how this is changing to meet and exceed the expectations of today's consumer.

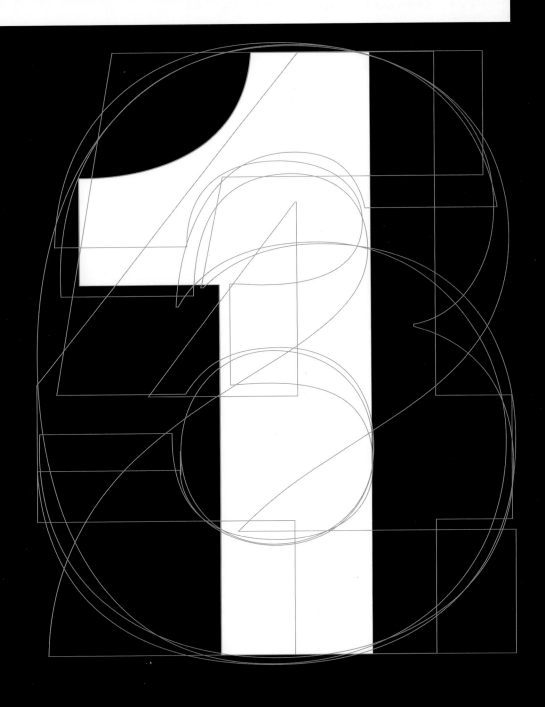

Retailing used to be a fairly straightforward affair; you opened a shop and sold goods that people wanted to buy, sometimes at a regulated price and hence a guaranteed profit. In some respects the Oxford English Dictionary is perhaps a little simplistic and needs updating on this point:

: **OXFORD ENGLISH DICTIONARY: RETAIL**

The sale of goods to the public in relatively small quantities for use or consumption rather than for resale.

The modern retail landscape is a far cry from this and unless you are selling ultra-desirable items such as the Hermes Birkin Handbag, which takes 18 hours to craft and has a waiting list to purchase, you have to excite and engage with your customers across a number of platforms. You have to help them love you and keep loving you; it's a relationship, something that needs to be maintained and constantly nurtured.

: **YASUSCHI KUSUME: INNOVATION AND CREATIVE MANAGER, IKEA**

'Much as two partners offer unconditional love to their children, a "loved" brand offers unconditional love to its specific audience.'

One of the key drivers for modern consumers is information; for retailers, it's knowledge. This is a potent mix and puts the ball firmly in the customer's hands; they can compare such factors as price, availability, customisation and desirability all from the comfort of their own home or increasingly, from anywhere they choose via their mobile device. This has allowed many items to be treated as tradable commodities where price is sometimes the sole driver – a good example of this might be books and music and, to an increasing degree, food shopping. However this doesn't necessarily mean the decline of cinemas, which have gained in popularity, nor the disappearance of book and record stores, which have changed to meet specific customer needs.

There are strong demographic changes which will continue to influence retail in the future, in particular emerging groups such as Millennials (those born between 1981 and 1994) and Generation Z (those born after 1995). These generations are comfortable with technology and will use this extensively to shop, both for comparison and inspiration. However a recent survey by global real estate company CBRE found that 70% of their purchases take place in store.

Figure 1.1 **HE BIRKIN HANDBAG BY HERMES** The quality and craftsmanship helps create a desirable item which customers are prepared to pay a premium price for. © rune hellestad/Corbis via Getty Images

Figure 1.2 **HOW DO WE CHOOSE?** When confronted with a range of choices customers will use prior knowledge in addition to the information they are presented with within the store. They will tend to use sharply focussed information to make speedy decisions. © George Doyle/ Stockbyte via Getty Images

Figure 1.3 AMAZON BOOKSTORE, SEATTLE
Amazon has a range of physical stores to connect more directly with their customers. © George Rose/ Getty Images

MILLENNIALS MYTHS & REALITIES, CBRE 2016:

'Making purchases in a physical store is still the preferred means of shopping for the Millennnial generation and this is unlikely to change dramatically . . . (Millennials) like to shop in person with friends, family or others and they want the physical experience of seeing, touching, testing and trying out goods.'

This access to information coupled with a lack of loyalty and a move towards retail defining lifestyle has led to an incredibly dynamic global retail environment where customers have an unparalleled range of choice of both products and services as well as, more importantly for retail design, how and where they purchase product.

The interrelationship of online brands opening physical stores and vice versa is creating new possibilities for the retail designer. They are now part of an ever-expanding multidiscipline team encompassing a range of specific specialisms.

The role of the Retail Designer does not stand alone but is informed by a number of key professionals. Some of these may be 'in house' and others will be specialist consultants; all of these will have an influence on the design to a greater or lesser degree.

In the following sections we will look at how these elements are brought together to form an engaging retail experience.

Figure 1.4 **RETAIL DESIGN** For a successful retail environment, there are many specialisms and factors which need to be considered in the design of a retail store. The designer will form part of this team and will be expected to liaise with many of these specialists.

In some respects we are reaching a defining point in the relationship between the customer and the retailer. The gap between the two is ever narrowing as global communication, interaction and production become more integrated.

In mature retail markets customer behaviour is changing; there is a lack of loyalty coupled with an increasing trust of those brands which meet and particularly exceed our expectations.

The panoply of choice available means that customers are not just shopping for physical products; one of the key areas of growth has been that of experiences and services which may sometimes revolve around an immediate or future purchase. This allows customers to develop a new relationship with brands but also allows brands to connect with their customers in many different ways.

Retail stores are becoming much more than an inventory of products; they are now seen as brand spaces using a range of spatial techniques and technologies to create and communicate ever-changing narratives and stories to captivate and engage customers.

Sometimes this experience is directly related to interactivity and is in fact an integral part of the experience, such as the French DIY chain Leroy Merlin or the hosting of dinner parties by IKEA in their Dining Club concept.

This merging of experiences is a growing phenomenon which is not only sweeping retail stores but is now a strong presence in brand flagship stores, websites and is manifesting itself in many retail malls to provide a more sustainable destination. The retail store will be an integral part of this but will no longer be solely where customers purchase product, but where they learn and experience the brand as well as providing retailers with feedback.

Figure 1.5 SOCIAL GALLERY INSTALLATION, SAMSUNG 837 NY by Black Egg 2016 Samsung 837 is an interactive engagement space for the brand. This installation allows visitors to directly interact with the installation through social media.
© Echochamber

Figure 1.6 APPLE STORE, REGENT STREET, LONDON, by Foster + Partners 2016 The new breed of Apple stores is more muted and allows for a more restful and natural environment in which to learn about and interact with the products. The expression of the brand is more subtle, allowing the customers to immerse themselves and create their own experiences.

In particular the use of materials such as terrazzo, marble and bronze creates a warm and sophisticated environment which complements and enhances the technology.
© Leon Neal/Getty Images

What customers are also seeking are levels of experience and engagement from other sectors such as the hospitality sector fed into their retail experiences. Hence we are seeing higher levels of customer service as part of the in store experience.

DAVID DALZIEL, DALZIEL AND POW:

'Wherever customers encounter you, online or instore, you need to present that "one brand space", that seamless brand experience.'

Figure 1.7 LEROY MERLIN, FRANCE: Dalziel & Pow 2015 This DIY retailer allows customers to try out products and also provides instruction in basic home construction tasks, letting customers gain knowledge of the product prior to purchasing. © Dalziel & Pow

**Figures 1.8, 1.9 and 1.10 PRIMARK
FLAGSHIP, MADRID: Dalziel & Pow
2015** Primark produces affordable fashion for
a wide range of customers through its stores
rather than online; it is particularly popular
with young people on a budget. Dalziel & Pow
took their existing traditional store format and
created a range of flagship stores which were
then used as a template for a roll-out into High
Street situations.

The space was sensitively restored using
traditional techniques with site-specific art
installations commissioned by local artists. It
has a sense of calm and wonder, enhanced by
seating and recharging areas giving customers
places to pause, allowing customers to gain
a new perspective of the brand; no wonder
that it is referred to as an 'Immersive Urban
Sanctuary'.

Breathing new life into a historic Madrid
building, this flagship store for Primark mixes
pioneering digital design with art installations
to create an urban sanctuary for customers.
The centerpiece is a 360-degree cinematic
experience in the octagonal atrium space where
11 interconnected transparent screens play
bespoke content and audio. © Dalziel & Pow

A key area of growth in retail,
particularly in fashion, is an area termed
Affordable Luxury. Consumers love
brands but they also love a bargain and
this apparent dichotomy has opened
up a range of possibilities for retailers
spawning a range of responses which
might be considered as Luxury *with*
Value.

It is now a familiar sight to see models
in fashion shoots wearing high-end
Prada twinned with High Street brands
and this has created an expectation
of service and particularly store
environment with all customers.
This has resulted in even mid-price
brands opening flagship stores and
sponsorships which position their
brand above their price point, providing
their customers with a new level of
experience.

Figure 1.11 COS & OTHER STORIES, US As part of their strategy to reach other market segments, the Swedish fashion brand H&M have developed the store COS together with '& Other Stories' which speak to a more upmarket sophisticated consumer. The stores include elements of Scandinavian design such as iconic pieces of furniture. © View Pictures/UIG via Getty Images

Many high-end retailers have extended their customer range by releasing diffusion ranges which are intended to maintain the cache of the brand but at a lower price point. They are aimed as non-competitive with existing brands but offer the opportunity to trade up within the brand family. This fluidity has been exploited by H&M through COS and their & Other Stories brands who sell stylish clothes at a higher price point than their owner brand – the reverse of the preceding idea.

Where are people shopping?

Through the use of a range of mobile technologies and apps consumers can now shop when they like and where they like with retail systems rapidly improving to make this a reality. Shopping is becoming a seamless experience across a range of platforms but is also allowing customers to merge experiences with other activities such as eating, entertainment and leisure.

: **RICHARD BENNET, DALZIEL AND POW**

'Engaging brands are realising that one-size-fits-all no longer works; they should consider more tailored offers and capsule formats to target a specific consumer in a certain location.'

This has resulted in retailers moving away from some areas such as downtown and regional malls to niche areas, boutique department stores and

Figure 1.12 J CREW Outfitter J Crew inhabited this vintage Liquor Store concept in Tribeca, NY to create a unique retail experience. Here the obvious branding is very low key, relying on the host environment to create a unique customer experience. © J. Crew

innovative malls and even multi-brand stores which attract a wider range of customers. In some cases they might take over an existing store, which targets a specific demographic, and retail out of this almost unchanged.

In 2016 Steve Howard, Head of Sustainability at IKEA, caused a debate by suggesting that in the West we have reached 'peak stuff' and that in the future we would recycle rather than own things. IKEA has responded to this by working to provide a more circular attitude to retailing, inspiring and empowering their customers rather than just selling them flat pack furniture.

Figure 1.13 IKEA DINING CLUB, 2015 Furniture retailer IKEA has developed a number of initiatives which enable them to connect with and get closer to their customers. These range from examples such as their Dining Clubs through to apartments and hotels. This example in London's Shoreditch allowed customers to book three-hour slots where they could learn about cooking Scandinavian-inspired dishes and then host a dinner party for up to 19 guests. This came from research which revealed that over one third of people in the UK had neither the space nor the time to host a dinner party. © Dan Kitwood/Getty Images

Originally founded by Gordon Selfridge in 1908, Selfridges occupies an entire block of Oxford Street, London and was the West End's biggest department store. The façade, with its richly decorated neoclassical columns and imposing main entrance, has been described as an 'extraordinary temple of the retail business'.

During the last twenty years Selfridges has gone through a process of total reinvention starting in 1996 with the appointment of Vittorio Radice as managing director. He set about an extensive programme of store refurbishments and expansion, but more importantly created strong links with leading luxury brands and instigated a series of events throughout the year to attract shoppers.

This has evolved into a complete customer experience encompassing enticing display windows, imaginative product stories and environments through to celebrity-endorsed events and promotions.

'People visit Selfridges for the experience, for the sense of Fun and for the customer service'.

ANNE PITCHER, MANAGING DIRECTOR, SELFRIDGES

Selfridges brings together a strong customer experience, great brands together with events, a strong social media presence and a seamless online experience to provide a powerful global retail presence.

'We're about curating, so we like to offer our customers things they don't know they want yet.'

SIMON FORSTER, OMNICHANNEL DIRECTOR, SELFRIDGES

1.14 (below) SELFRIDGES WINDOW DISPLAY Customers are enticed into the store by frequently changing window displays which usually reflect seasonal events. © Ben Pruchnie/Getty Images

1.15 (opposite) THE FRAGRANCE LAB, SELFRIDGES, CAMPAIGN, 2014 Areas such The Fragrance Lab have created destinations not only within the store but have become 'must visit' places for shoppers the world over. This strong physical presence is now being exploited through the retailer's Omnichannel presence. © Campaign creative Ltd

1.16 SELFRIDGES EVENT Selfridges host a range of events which are both promotional and aspirational and allows customers to identify with the celebrity endorsements of the brands that it sells. © David M. Benett/Getty Images

We are all consumers and we like to think that we know what we want and that we purchase products using a logical framework which responds to our wants and needs. We are probably aware of advertising and respond to this in what we consider to be a measured way, filtering the information as required. What we are probably less aware of is the range of techniques and psychology that retailers employ to gain our attention and influence our purchasing habits.

The retail experience has changed radically over the last few years with the rise of both the informed consumer and the emotional brand. We are now moving inexorably from brands as a point of difference to that of a continuing relationship. The concept of the retail experience is not a single entity but can be divided into a series of defined stages each of which requires careful attention and management from the designers, and understanding of what the users of that process will be experiencing.

Figure 1.17 **STAGES OF EXPERIENCE:** The five key stages of the retail experience are described in the diagram (Figure 1.17) together with photographs illustrating an example from a particular retail site. Although these should flow into a seamless overall experience it is important that the customers' needs and expectations are met during each stage in their journey.
© Stephen Anderson. Photos BDP

Figure 1.18 **IMPLEMENTATION OF EXPERIENCE:** This initial layout begins to develop the areas of experience for a proposed store design. This is used to shape the final layouts to deliver the anticipated experience based on application of the five key stages in Figure 1.17.
© Path Design

Anticipation	Recognition	Welcome	Immersion	Reflection

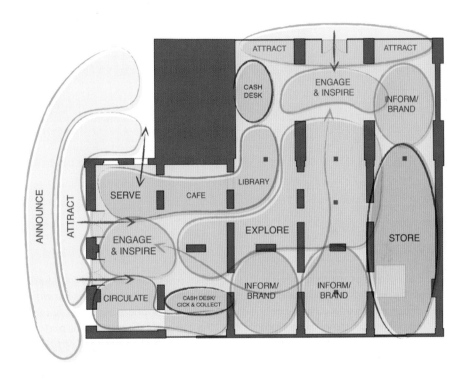

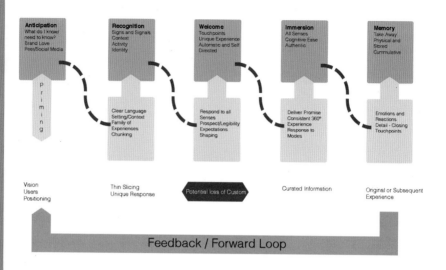

As we have seen previously it is also clear that the physical design of a store is responsible for only part of the customer experience, along with many other elements such as marketing and brand profile being integral parts of the overall experience. These need to be managed at each stage of the process such that there will be specific messages communicated by the brand and environment which will elicit specific responses from the users. In a well-designed system these will be known and predictable but where the design of any part of the system is poor, negative responses can result. In any system there are specific situations known as touchpoints where it is important that the customers' expectations and the experience are aligned.

These aspects need to be considered in the early stages of the design development and it is important that the designer recognizes the journey that the customer should take and how they navigate the space. The design should incorporate clearly defined elements with touchpoints, interaction areas and allow for the appropriate staff interface with customers.

Figure 1.19 (opposite) **THE RETAIL JOURNEY: KEY POINTS, Stephen Anderson 2016:** We can examine the stages of a retail experience in more detail which will allow us to highlight the important decisions which might be faced at each stage both from the customer and retailer perspectives. The diagram in Figure 1.19 details some of the aspects which define customer behaviour at each stage and those that might be considered if the experience fails to meet the customers' expectations. These are sometimes referred to as Fail or Pain Points. © Stephen Anderson

1.20 CONCEPT FOR ARGOS DIGITAL STORE, Dalziel & Pow 2013: At this early stage of the design the key elements of the store are arranged with purpose to create an engaging customer experience. © Dalziel & Pow

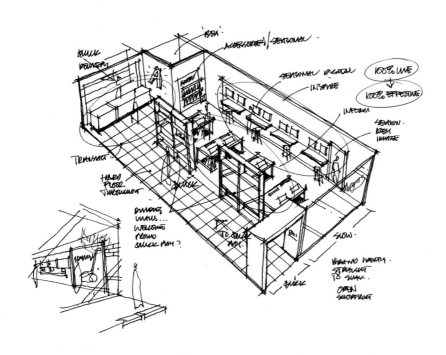

Not only do we engage with the store environment as a series of experiences, we also may approach it in a different frame of mind or mode which may be dependent on the time of day or our purchasing intentions.

On a basic level our purchasing intentions will be dependant on factors such as:

Time of Day

We shop differently at the weekend than, say, at lunchtime

Seasonal

Events such as holiday periods

Planned or Unplanned Visit

This may depend on the amount of in store information we require

Type of Product

Items such as Food, White Goods and Clothing are predominately bought in store.

These can be developed to create more useful ways of evaluating our shopping intentions.

However research has shown that we don't always shop in the same frame of mind or with the same intentions but in a variety of modes. We respond differently to the shopping environment depending which mode we are shopping in. Ideally the needs of each mode will be met and satisfied in the design of the retail space.

These modes are not necessarily fixed with regards to customer demographics as in say the case of the ethical consumer, but they may change based around what we are expecting from a particular brand or purchasing decision.

Food shopping is a good example here. Food used to be purchased in a big shop as a considered mode of shopping. The trend today is for more frequent visits to purchase when required, which may be in either a convenience or impulse mode.

Shopping Modes

Modes

Figure 1.21 SHOPPING MODES These illustrate some of modes in which we shop; these are not necessarily fixed and may vary depending on a variety of factors.

This can be broken down to provide the designer with a simple flow diagram which allows them to examine in more detail how they might satisfy the needs of each particular mode.

Figures 1.22, 1.23 and 1.24 MAST, LOS ANGELES: 2016 Mast Brothers is a New York-based chocolate maker founded by pioneering brothers Rick and Michael Mast in 2007. The chocolate is produced with obsessive attention to detail, meticulous craftsmanship, groundbreaking innovation and inspirational simplicity.

In this store the product is treated as a precious commodity and the link between the ingredients and the product tell a story of care and attention to detail.

This is particularly evident in the displays of the product and its ingredients. © Jessie Webster via Camron PR

Small is meaningful

In recent years we have seen the rise of the specialist consumer: one who cares intensely about the products they buy and the places where they purchase these products, forming a strong individual bond. They are looking for health and freshness and are particularly interested in the process, production and ingredients of the products they purchase and are manifested in producers such as artisan bakers, craft beer, coffee and tea houses.

Perhaps as a reaction to the increased connectedness and digitization of people's lives there has been a strong move towards authenticity and provenance of products and more especially experiences. The main focus of this has been in the areas of food and beverage which has manifested itself in the design of experiences that engage all of the senses and are specific to place and product.

It is interesting that these experiences are grounded in authenticity and have a high level of customer engagement. These are specifically those characteristics that cannot be easily reproduced online; they are also very effective in creating a powerful memory of the product which can drive online sales. Most of the original stores are single outlets or small chains, where they pride and maintain their individual experiences and products. However large brands are increasingly looking at this expanding market and are beginning to acquire these brands into their portfolios. They are using these either to present a different face of the brand or allowing customers to reconnect with their original brand messages.

> **HOWARD SCHULTZ, STARBUCKS CEO**
>
> 'Every Starbucks store is carefully designed to enhance the quality of everything the customers see, touch, smell, or taste.'

Figure 1.25 STARBUCKS RESERVE ROASTERY, SEATTLE This has been developed by Starbucks to create an image of authenticity and an opportunity to allow customers to connect with the values of the brand. It also aligns the brand with the artisan coffee producers that are changing the face of how we perceive the coffee experience. © David Ryder/Bloomberg via Getty Images

The end of the vanilla experience

Traditionally larger global brands have adopted a strategy of consistency of message to their customers across a range of markets. This has sometimes resulted in a bland homogenous experience with little relevance to local context. In an increasingly competitive marketplace and especially through the emergence of developing local brands and a desire from consumers for a customized experience, retailers have revisited the old adage of 'Thinking globally but acting locally', an attempt to provide an authentic 'local' experience in differing global markets. This has moved from purely product-based offers; McDonalds famously tailors its products in markets such as India where the Big Mac is a Chicken Maharaja Mac, through to the overall environmental experience.

Increasingly global brands in particular are differentiating themselves through design and the use of recognized architects, designers and even artists to create exciting and innovative environments that challenge consumer expectations of their more mainstream identity.

HARVARD BUSINESS REVIEW 2004

'. . . consumers expect global brands to tell their myths from the particular places that are associated with the brand. For Nestlé to spin a credible myth about food, the myth must be set in the Swiss mountains, because that is where people imagine the brand hails from.'

Figures 1.26 and 1.27
McDONALD'S RESTAURANT, CHAMPS ELYSEES, PARIS, Patrick Norguet Architects 2016 Here the designer has quite specifically created an environment that not only provides relevance to the local market and consumer but also allows customers to view the brand in a completely fresh light.
Simple materials such as concrete, sheet metal and industrial metal mesh contrast with ceiling mounted light boxes covered with colourful vinyls. This creates a very contemporary feel and an uncompromisingly urban experience. © Renaud Callebaut via Patrick Norguet

We have never had more choice in terms of product, experience and convenience; however this can also lead to confusion and lack of fulfilment through potential conflicting desires and aspirations. In an age of increasing connectivity and prosperity we are looking for a customized response to our needs and the physical manifestation first identified in *The Long Tail* by Chris Anderson. Anderson suggests that rather than a (relatively) few brands reaching a wide range of customers there will be a larger number each reaching a smaller, more targeted number of customers.

With consumer spending on culture and recreation rising we are rapidly moving from buying product to consuming experiences. However this may be a little simplistic and it might be more accurate to say we may be moving to a model of 'engaged consumption'.

This will continue its direct impact of retail behaviour and design on real estate and will lead to more flexible leasing terms (perhaps based on intangibles rather than turnover or size), smaller more flexible stores, speciality outlets and flash stores or pop ups.

The seamless merging of physical and digital retail will continue to offer customers an ever-increasing number of ways in which to access and purchase products; omni channel retail will continue to provide opportunities for both customers and retailers to buy and sell products. Customers will be looking for a variety of experiences from physical retail which will increasingly focus towards those which cannot be easily replicated online or digitally.

> **CHRIS ANDERSON, AUTHOR OF THE LONG TAIL, 2004.**
>
> 'When consumers are offered infinite choice, the true shape of demand is revealed. People gravitate towards niches because they satisfy narrow interests better, and in one aspect of our life or another we all have some narrow interest.'

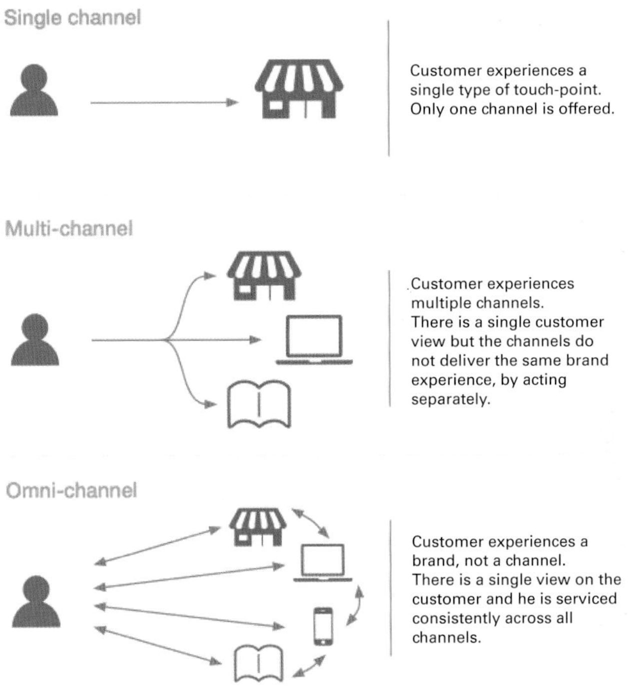

Single channel

Customer experiences a single type of touch-point. Only one channel is offered.

Multi-channel

Customer experiences multiple channels. There is a single customer view but the channels do not deliver the same brand experience, by acting separately.

Omni-channel

Customer experiences a brand, not a channel. There is a single view on the customer and he is serviced consistently across all channels.

Figure 1.28 **OMNI CHANNEL RETAILING** The linking of technologies and channels creates new possibilities for retailers to engage with their customers in new and different ways. Taken from The Future Trend in Fashion and Luxury Industry sourced from https://fashionbi.com/research.

STEPHEN ARMSTRONG, FUTURE OF RETAIL 2016

'Omnichannel, in its simplest definition, is a complete combination of in-store and online, using every single channel from mobile and social to personal shopper and in-store events.

This artful blend of new tech and old stone is at the heart of the rise of omnichannel retailing in the age of 'me-commerce' where the consumer is boss.'

Soft technology

The store environment has become a network of opportunities to shop and for many people may not be their first engagement with the brand. They will expect an enhanced experience but also a wide-ranging and connected one which allows the retailer to build on existing relationships.

In the future stores will use technologies such as in-store GPS and wi-fi to track customer movements and actions. This will allow them to provide a tailored customized response and may allow customers to find the product they are looking at by scanning the barcode or even just touching the product. If, for example the size or colour is not available in-store this can be ordered in real time for delivery when the customer gets home.

Technologies such as iBeacon and Google positioning systems allow retailers to connect with their customers in store by tracking their position. This allows for customisation of the experience through providing discount offers, new product launches and general lifestyle information. Many retailers are trying a variety of dynamic or fluid pricing strategies, something borrowed from the sports and entertainment industries. This is based on a combination of customer loyalty programmes and information that the retailer may hold about the customer such as salary or where they live.

For Retail Design this has an impact in terms of integration of technology and flexibility for change out and upgrading and should be considered at the initial concept stage and integrated within planning and store design.

Technology will play an increasingly meaningful role in our retail experience and it will become more ubiquitous and invisible, used as an enabler for stronger relationships and the creation of customer communities.

: **LINDIE KRAMERS, BRAND DIRECTOR, KINNERSLEY KENT DESIGN**

'The store of the future will have many fully integrated channels, each being a seamless extension of the other – full integration will be a convenience, just the norm."

Figure 1.29 ADIDAS, ENDLESS AISLE TECHNOLOGY The system allows customers to scan the whole range of products, some of which may not be displayed in-store at that time. It also includes opportunities for customisation and unique material or colour combinations. © Connected Retail Ltd

Figure 1.30 COOP SUPERMARKET OF THE FUTURE, MILAN 2015 This trail concept by coop Italy is an attempt to recreate the feeling of a street marketplace linked to a range of 'smart' technologies to appeal to modern consumers.

The concept allows customers to connect with suppliers and to learn the provenance of what they are purchasing.

The Supermarket of the Future helps to remove the barriers between food producers and consumers and allows them to have a more direct relationship with food. This uses a range of new technology, including touch screen displays providing additional information such as nutritional information, and interactive showcases with LED sensors that provide visitors with information on the production, consumption and distribution of food in the future. © Echochamber

In this book each chapter will contain a series of exercises which will help you to explore, test and gain a greater understanding of the topics covered. Many of these will be based on observation and recording; there are also some basic notes which are common to all of the exercises in this book.

Observation and research methods

During site visits you are encouraged to use a variety of methods of recording what you observe; some of these are listed as follows.

User Behaviours

There are a few methods that you might adopt:

- A Day in the Life

  Look at how people use the space during different periods of the day; lunchtime will be very different from mid-afternoon. This can be mapped on a timeline.

- Camera or Sketch Journal

  Try to record your experiences as a reflective journal, and record what you think works well and where any 'fail points' occur. Don't forget to ask for the owner's permission if you take photographs

- Observation Log

  Go through the actions of, say, buying a product; visualize your findings in a way that communicates the steps and experiences that you went through. Was the process intuitive? How long did you have to wait? What was working well? What was not?

  Look at the graphic design and branding; materials, colour and light; products, objects and artefacts (for example, cups, jugs, coffee machines, art etc); and produce (what is sold and how it is displayed and served to the customer).

Observe ▶ Record ▶ Action

Recording and communicating

Gather together your research information and consider the following from observations from the sites that you visited:

You should record these using sketches, photographs and artefacts; communicate these clearly through diagrams and perhaps collage.

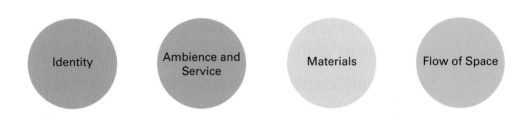

Exercises for this chapter

Customer Blueprints

Blueprinting an experience is an excellent way of either mapping an experience that you have witnessed or testing a proposed concept you may wish to develop.

Start by considering the experience that you wish to create and write down every aspect of that process required. A good idea is to write these on Post-it notes and then arrange these on a desk or wall. Add more if ideas come to mind.

Next you should organize these into a logical sequence which might be one or all of the following:

1. The stages of experience as indicated on page 23

2. Consider how the process may vary throughout times of the day or seasonal aspects.

3. You might also look at the idea of shopping modes – how will different users relate to the experience?

4. Look at how users such as customers, staff, technology and display interact with the process to create an experience.

5. Photograph and draw your ideas, try to develop a diagram in line with that on page 23.

Branding is a term used extensively in retail to mean a systemized approach to form and develop relationships between customers and a product or company. There are a range of views and methods of how to apply this, the key ones of which are explored in this chapter.

We can all identify with brands that are familiar to us and part of our everyday life. But how does a brand translate from two dimensions into the volume of an interior space? The answer can be complex and forms the basis of the keystone of the design process; understanding a brand is one of the most important aspects of the retail designer's role. In most interior design, understanding the building is the starting point and subject of investigation. In retail, however, the brand is the starting point and the building or site will reinforce this.

THIS CHAPTER will examine some key aspects of how the brand and identity of a product, service or experience shape the relationship between retailers and consumers and how the retail space communicates this. This will help set the scene and context for the practice of retail design and explore how this is changing to meet and exceed the expectations of today's consumer.

The concept of branding is intrinsically linked with advertising, marketing and, as we have seen in the previous chapter, responding to the subconscious aspirations of the consumer. A brand can be a product, a person or a logo – anything that can be bought and sold, such as an idea or artefact, can be branded.

Branding is an attempt to harness these associations in order for the business to perform better. It is evident that brands possess values that distinguish them from their competitors and is interesting to consider why we buy a branded product over a supermarket-named equivalent at a lower price. What makes us believe that the contents of the tin are of a better quality?

Some brands have crossed boundaries in becoming the name associated with the product. For instance, a tablet computer is most commonly called an iPad; at a bar we ask for Coke (Coca-Cola) rather than Pepsi; brands have even become verbs, such as to Google something. The power of the brand is evident in our everyday lives and our language is cluttered with brand references.

Through marketing and advertising, the image of the brand is identified and sold to the particular groups or market segments to which it is aimed. The brand can be defined by analysing its core values through understanding the product, communicating it to the right consumer audience and understanding that audience, and finally matching the product to the physical environment.

In retail terms, the store experience is built around the values of the brand and the products sold within it. The interior emulates the aspirations of the brand values and qualities to enhance the relationship between the space and the message. Typically the brand will be consistent – from the visual style through the experience and service to the product range, whether diverse or focused, within the interior. However, there is a growing tendency for brands to project messages which uniquely respond to a particular segment or culture and these may be delivered in different ways in a variety of sites.

: **THE POWER OF BRANDING – DESIGN COUNCIL (UK)**

'a brand is a set of associations that a person (or group of people) makes with a company, product, service, individual or organization.'

Figure 2.1 **PRIMARK FLAGSHIP, MADRID: Dalziel & Pow 2015** This striking environment appeals to the key Primark demographic as well as responding to its specific location. © Dalziel & Pow

Evolution of branding

Over the years the idea of what a brand is has changed from that of simple differentiation by name through to today's use of the brand to form an emotional attachment or relationship. This is largely due to how the brand is expressed and communicated across an ever-widening range of channels from the virtual to the physical and vice versa.

The earliest examples of branding can be traced back as far as the 1880s when logos began to appear on food packages such as Campbell's soup, Coca-Cola and Lyle's Golden Syrup. The first examples of branding were simply that of a name attached to the product to differentiate it and provide a guarantee of quality and provenance.

In the mid-twentieth century organizations began to adjust the laws of advertising to describe their business and function, rather than products, and the term 'brand identity' became mainstream in corporate language.

The concept of branding developed globally in the 1980s, following a downturn in sales, largely through lack of quality control with such famous brands as Levi's and Harley Davidson. Moving production overseas to places such as China and India for a fraction of the cost made good economic sense, but this led to problems of supply chain management and quality.

Brands such as Nike realized this at an early stage in their development; their founder and CEO Phil Knight recognized the huge potential of creating an authentic sports brand whilst controlling manufacturing costs through global production.

This strong emotional attachment allows brands to connect with their customers in a relationship of mutual benefit, learning from each other and growing together.

Since the 1990s there has been a revolution in branding, largely fuelled by a mixture of interconnectivity, communication and social media. This has allowed brands to connect with people in ever more meaningful and intimate ways; this also allows for a certain self-selection where the key audience 'gets' the messages which others might miss or not be attracted to.

In contrast to this there has been a democratization of brands where retailers such as Muji describe themselves as 'no brand'. This originated in Japan where their values are communicated in subtle ways through the simplicity and quality of their products, store ambience and displays.

The advent of social media and the rise of personal branding and celebrity has allowed brands to expand their reach rapidly both in terms of geographic spread and speed of communication. This has changed the traditional role of advertising whereby many brands can

Figure 2.2 EARLY BRAND ADVERTISING
Early examples of branding tended to differentiate and create associations through the use of a recognisable name and image.
© Library of Congress/Corbis/VCG via Getty Images

> **PHIL KNIGHT, NIKE**
>
> 'Nike is "a sports company"; its mission is not to sell shoes but to "enhance people's lives through sports and fitness" and to keep "the magic of sports alive".'

Figure 2.3 **MUJI STORE, NEW YORK** Simple displays of quality products exemplify the Muji brand as 'no brand'. © James Leynse/Corbis via Getty Images

now circumvent this and speak directly to their customers. This relationship is further strengthened by the multitude of reviews, likes and favourites displayed on a range of influential websites, blogs and media platforms such as Instagram, Twitter and Facebook.

Brand relationships

In an increasingly connected and choice-saturated world we need help to make the right choices, someone we can trust to deliver goods and services to match our needs, increasingly trusting brands more than we do some existing institutions.

In this open environment, emerging brands have a unique opportunity to work with their brand through their customers to deliver their message, this allows them to play with the ideas of the brand with their customers.

PAUL NICHOLSON, CHALK ARCHITECTURE

'The Small Batch experience touches each of these activities one way or another depending on which site you visit. We were clear from the start the design of the branding and the interior needed to evoke a sense of the story of coffee, and that this underpins the Small Batch concept.'

Figure 2.4 **SMALL BATCH COFFEE, BRIGHTON, Chalk Architecture, 2010** Here the idea of the brand is expressed as authentic, being burnt into the timber of a chair denoting authenticity and care in production, some of the company's core values. © Jim Stephenson / www.clickclickjim.com

Every brand identity is formed by defining the main principles behind its meaning. As well as considering the product and its environment, it is important to maintain a vision of how to establish a brand and how it stands alongside its competitors. Those brands that stay true to their brand values are able to survive and conquer in a ferociously competitive world.

There are many views on branding and what the key elements are; next we have cited some of the principles of a brand under the following headings:

Big idea This is the uniting concept or idea of the brand, holding everything together; there are a number of elements which help support this. Some of the questions you might ask here: What is your offer? How do you stand out? What do you do that is different? What are my customers looking for?

Vision This should describe where you want to be, sometimes referred to as mission.

Values These are what you stand for and share with your customers, employees and other stakeholders. It may also refer to your moral and ethical position.

Personality This communicates aspects such as your tone of voice, graphic and visual language.

Storytelling An increasingly popular way of communicating the unique aspects of your brand, how it is different and what it means to its customers.

Essence The essence identifies what is at the heart of the business and the nature of the work. These are the most important features of the organization.

Strange attractor The success of many brands is in the unknown and the additional offers that can be made under a brand. It is important to question what else people are looking for from the brand.

Culture Who is the market/consumer/user and what does it feel like to be part of this culture?

WALLY OLINS

'. . . to be really effective you have to be able to sense the brand. You may even be able to touch it and feel it. So that it manifests the core idea.'

Figure 2.5
**TIMES SQUARE,
New York** Competing
brands vie for
customers' attention;
simple recognizable
messages need to be
communicated and
received. © Brigitte
Blättler via Getty

Figure 2.6
**HANDLEBAR
COFFEE, SINGAPORE**
There is no disputing
the strong personality
behind this small
individual coffee outlet;
this is a man living
his brand. © Stephen
Anderson

: **CREATIVE DIRECTOR ALASDHAIR WILLIS**

'The Regent Street flagship store opened in 2014 and was the first opportunity for the Hunter customer to enter the home of this iconic British brand. Lifting iconic references from the British countryside and appropriating them for the urban environment, it shows Hunter's take on the traditional store concept designed to appeal to our diverse customer base.'

**Figures 2.7, 2.8 and 2.9 HUNTER FLAGSHIP,
REGENT STREET, LONDON, In House design with
implementation by Checkland Kindleysides, 2015** The
Hunter Flagship in Regent Street, London is the first
expression of the brand in a retail environment.

There are references to the British countryside with the
grey-tinted Douglas fir rafters of a barn. This is further
reinforced through the display of gabion dry stone walls
forming the backdrop to a wall of Original Wellington boots,
which were first introduced in 1956. © Hunter Boots Ltd

In order to develop or reinvent a brand, the organization involved will go through a series of processes to gain an understanding of the brand's nature or, in the case of reinvention, to consider what is not working.

Organizations often employ brand consultants to manage this process, as they may not have the expertise in-house. There are various stages involved. The first stage is to conduct research and analysis to investigate the nature of the organization and its characteristics. This is done through auditing the organization's existing position in terms of retail space, products or facilities, for example. Also at this point, the organization may look to examine its main competitors in order to define their place in the market. The information generated during this initial stage then goes on to inform the development of the brand and to create a core idea from which everything about the organization can be derived.

The next stage sees the involvement of the design team as they contextualize the meanings behind the core ideas, questioning how the brand looks and feels. This would be demonstrated through graphic mood and lifestyle boards as a starting point. Once the feel and look is established and agreed on between designer and client, a style can be established that will work for both the graphic and interior design. This is a good example of how graphic designers and interior designers work together. Sometimes this process includes the development of a new name or logo, or working with a style that already exists; naming consultants may be employed for this. During the graphic design process, all kinds of decisions are made as to how the brand will appear throughout the experience. Once the designs have been agreed, the brand guidelines are established in a manual that is put together by the graphic designer. The guidelines are an important document that is given to all contractors involved in advertising and signage so that consistency is kept throughout the implementation stage. The guidelines include logo information, colour references, typeface and imagery, as well as examples of how to set out different types of signage, stationery and other communication tools. This manual also informs the graphic quality and finishes for the interior spaces.

Branding the interior

Imagine a shell of a building that is a blank canvas with neutral walls, floors and ceilings. Think of a well-known brand and the associated colour, pattern, logo, sound or scent. Understand the product and who might buy it. Analyse the lifestyle of someone who would use this brand: What car do they drive? Where do they live? How much money do they earn? And most importantly, what would they expect from a retail experience? All of these questions form the basis from which to develop a concept that will underpin the interior scheme.

: ALASDAIR LENNOX, FITCH DESIGN, UK

'There's a difference between a branded environment and a brand experience. A branded environment is where the colours and the shapes and the forms all point towards brand identity.

What we do is brand experience . . . it's the vibe, the ambience, the experience and how you introduce it.'

The interior scheme often takes its lead from the graphic guidelines, through understanding the aspirations of the end-user and through analysing the competition. This information is portrayed through visual research or 'mood boards' (images and photographs retrieved from books or journals that explain clearly the thought process and ideas of the design team) but will be interior-orientated rather than graphically based. The key features of the visual research are then extracted into 'stories' that lead to explicit ideas about what the interior design scheme could be and how the graphic identity would impact on the space. From this process, an interior concept is born.

Concept interpretation

The concept is then tested in the interior space through visual storyboards that may contain adjacency and circulation plans, animated sketch visuals and samples of material finishes. It is common for different schemes to emerge at this time, all of which will be presented to the client. The client and designer then work together to come to a conclusive design idea: this may result clearly from just one of the presented concepts or may result from a combination of all the potential concepts. Once the concept has been decided, the designer then works on the detail of the design. This process builds with each client meeting until a conclusion is reached and a set of drawings can be produced in the form of a manual.

Delivering the scheme

Once a design concept has been agreed on between client and designer, a programme is developed to deliver the interior into the client's existing or new sites. This may be an individual site or a 'roll out' – reproducing the same interior across different sites.

In the case of multiple sites, a manual will be prepared by the design team which contains all of the elements of the design, describing ways to adapt the scheme for different types of site. A variety of layouts and elevational configurations are drawn up, as well as detailed drawings for every fixture and fitting, a finishes schedule and a lighting scheme.

Sometimes the designer's role ends there and the information is handed over to the client, who in turn employs a contractor to oversee and implement the design in each store. On other occasions, the designer will work with the client and contractors to prepare separate drawing packages for each site, using the manual as a guide for consistency. This would entail dealing with local authority planning departments and making site visits. This would usually be at the start of a project, midway through the programme, and

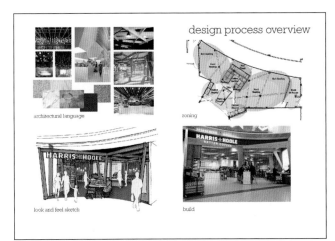

design process overview

architectural language

zoning

look and feel sketch

build

Figure 2.10 Harris & Hoole Concept, Path Design, 2016 This example shows how the design team have explored the brand in a specific location to produce a focussed response to the site. This includes exploration though simple visuals and proposed layouts. Diagrams © Path Design, photograph © Michael Fair Photography

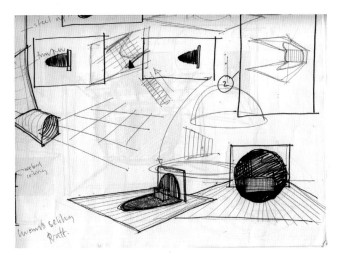

Figures 2.11 and 2.12 FULLCIRCLE FLAGSHIP STORE London, UK, 2008 The design for this flagship store is a literal interpretation of the Fullcircle brand. A 'floating' white, architectural box, set within the envelope of the original landlord's space, has been cut away to reveal a dramatic optical illusion that, when viewed from the shop entrance, describes a 12-metre-wide full circle at the rear of the store. The images shown here demonstrate the development of the design scheme, from sketch to final execution. © Alex Franklin via Brinkworth

to 'snag' the site, fixing final details, before handover at the end of the build. The designer would also liase with the contractor regarding any queries that may arise. The designer may also become involved with the visual merchandising of the store, although most large retailers have their own in-house team specifically tasked with dressing every store the same.

Building the interior

The design of a retail interior can be split into three broad areas in terms of design and particularly budget, and each may also have a very specific function. Approximately 70 per cent of the client's budget would be spent on the architecture of the building, meaning repair or structural alteration work of the building fabric, electrical supplies and environmental services as well as key elements such as flooring, ceilings and lighting. These elements are critical to the interior structure but some would not necessarily be apparent to the customer. They must, however, have the potential to last up to 20 years, as this may be the length of lease that the client commits to.

Secondly, the fixtures and fittings to display the merchandise and make the store function would cost approximately 20 per cent of the client's budget and would have a lifespan of around six years. These are an important part of the customers' experience although not all of these may be immediately visible.

The final 10 per cent of the budget pays for the visual branded elements of the scheme, through graphic communication, finish (colour, pattern or texture for instance), logos displayed where possible, music or scent. This is the critical element that finally dresses the space and portrays the lifestyle of the brand. These elements may be changed every season, week or day if fashion and trend demands it and they mimic the key message of the moment. The retail store is under constant reinvention.

> **RASSHIED DIN**
>
> The retail designer's task is to combine elements of psychology, technology and ergonomics with the retailer's knowledge of the market.

Figures 2.13, 2.14, 2.15 and 2.16 VERTU STORE Tokyo DESIGNER KLEIN DYTHAM ARCHITECTURE, 2011 From the arrival at this new showroom the shopfront and especially the profiled façade all add to the luxurious, opulent feel of the brand. The approach was to create an interior that matched the sophistication and attention to detail of Vertu phones. The interior's elegantly restrained spaces translate the quality of materials and finishing apparent in the brand's products. © Shed

The way that brands communicate has changed rapidly as the adoption and integration of online and multi-channel retailing has increasingly overtaken physical sales. This has led to a fundamental shift in the way that brands communicate with their customers. The idea of brands communicating big messages to many people has been replaced with focussed messages to many people.

> : OLINS W, THE WOLFF OLINS GUIDE
> TO CORPORATE IDENTITY
>
> 'All organizations communicate all the time. Everything that they make or do or say – or don't say – is a form of communication.
>
> The totality of the way the organization presents itself and is seen to be can be called it's identity.'

In this section we will look at a variety of ways in which a brand is communicated through physical stores. These are usually sited in major retail positions, to allow access to the larger proportion of the world's consumers.

These examples highlight important aspects or trends which range from the more traditional flagship store through to concept stores and ideas of experience and curation.

Increasingly, brands are using their customers' insights into what they want the brand to become and this is manifesting itself in a variety of store

> : NEUMEIER M, THE BRAND GAP
>
> 'A brand is a person's gut feeling about a product, service or company. It is not what you say it is. It's what they say it is.'

formats which are generally either mobile or short stay and are referred to as pop up or flash stores.

Flagship store

The flagship has become the most influential and creative of retail spaces and has fuelled a fertile fusion of fashion and architectural design. These major brand stores tend to be implemented in the major retail areas in cities such as London, Paris and Milan.

One of the earliest flagship stores was the NikeTown concept which was first rolled out in Portland in 1990 close to the Nike campus in Beaverton. This was loosely based on a narrative developed from the film *Back to the Future* of 1985 and importantly provides an intensely choreographed experience using techniques from film and exhibition design. Originally conceived by Nike's in-house design team in conjunction with Borra architects, it was rolled out to several cities in the US and into five global locations.

In many ways this established the principle of the flagship as a platform for the visualization of the brand rather than a straightforward retail store. Research in the US has demonstrated that stores within a twenty-mile radius of a Nike flagship store experienced an uplift in their retail sales.

Figure 2.17 NIKETOWN LONDON, BDP with Nike Design, 1999. Nike used a strong narrative and recognizable interior elements to create the first flagship stores.

From this the idea, the flagship has expanded and evolved into a variety of configurations and interpretations. These will continue to develop and focus on the customer experience and engagement with the brand, together with the offer of customization of products and services as well as a testing ground for new ideas and directions of the brand. © BDP

: **REM KOOLHAAS**

'Shopping is a phenomenon that has "remained mysteriously invisible to the architectural eye . . . as one of the most critical and . . . important contributions to urban texture at this moment".'

Figures 2.18, 2.19 and 2.20 **PRADA EPICENTRE, OMA**

New York: This is one of several stores that OMA have created for this famous fashion brand. This space, almost anonymous from the outside, opens up to create a carefully controlled space where the brand can be expressed through product, performance and exhibition.

In this environment the product appears as a desirable and special object within the interior, which is frequently changed like an exhibition. This is further enhanced by a rolling programme of events for which the space is designed with extensive audio visual equipment and a retractable stage area. © OMA

Figure 2.21 **STARBUCKS, JAPAN, KENGO KUMA, 2011** This outlet is situated in Dazaifu, Fukuoka Prefecture in Japan, which is an area of great cultural significance. Rather than the traditional Starbucks format the design team responded to the site by using the idea of weaving timber sticks, referencing techniques from the traditional architecture of Japan and China. This creates a striking interior which presents the brand in a respectful yet contemporary framework. © Kengo Kuma

Concept store

This format can be used in a variety of ways: to test a new format or direction for the brand, appeal to a new customer group or to respond to a particular local context.

The concept can be tested over a range of sites and can be modified or customized to respond to the particular social, economic or cultural requirements.

Curated service

Increasing we are seeing brands merge or form alliances with each other where they see mutual benefit in terms of appealing to a particular group or demographic such as the recent collaboration between Gap and Virgin Hotels. The idea of personal service is perhaps not new but a recent collaboration between Rockar and car retailers such as Hyundai and Jaguar in the UK has taken this to another level. These stores have a high level of interactivity and customer engagement in the process and use crossover techniques from the hospitality sector. This allows the stores to locate in unexpected places such as shopping malls and high street situations.

DAVID DALZIEL, FOUNDER, DALZIEL & POW

'Ultimately, an engaging brand is a business that customers want to spend their time with, and their money on.'

57

Figure 2.22 ROCKAR HYUNDAI CARS, UK, DALZIEL & POW, 2016 This showroom focusses on the customer and is intended to demystify car buying, placing the 'showrooms' in central shopping hubs that blend the best of online and offline retail. Interactive touchscreen tablets allow customers to browse the product range independently, book test drives or even buy a car in a matter of minutes.

The store is defined by zones, tailored to different stages of the customer journey. A gallery-style 'white box' entrance displays a regular rotation of cars to attract passers-by, and then the 'create', 'educate' and 'inform' zones cater to all aspects of buying a car, from browsing and consultation to choosing bespoke finishes. The layout is inherently flexible with sliding walls allowing to create spaces for hosting private viewings and VIP launches. © Dalziel & Pow

Figure 2.23 TESLA SHOWROOM, UK The American company Tesla is also trialling similar formats; this example was found in the same mall as the Hyundai store. © Stephen Anderson

Pop-up

One of the key areas of growth in retail design in recent years has been that of the pop-up store, sometimes referred to as flash stores. These are highly targeted and short-lived environments which are closely linked to a brand's marketing strategy and new product development. By their very nature they have a slightly guerrilla feel to them and can be used to project a brand into a variety of unexpected sites and markets. These range from empty shop units to car parks and events such as design events and music festivals.

The main aspiration behind these stores is to parachute the message of the brand into a new location or channel or to target a particular group of potential customers.

Figure 2.24 **THE STORY, New York** STORY is a retail concept that takes the point of view of a magazine, changes like a gallery and sells things like a store. The store is changed out every four to eight weeks, completely reinventing itself, from the design to the merchandise. This provides a constantly changing focus so that literally every visit is different. © Story, New York

Figure 2.25 **NIKE PARK, Atlanta, 1996** Nike transformed this multi-storey car park adjacent to the Olympic site to create a brand experience; as they were not an official sponsor this positioned them as an edgy outsider brand. © Lutz Bongarts/Bongarts/Getty Images

Figure 2.26 **RAPHA, San Francisco, 2016** Cycling brand Rapha creates these innovative stores, which they refer to as 'Club Houses', around the world, focussing on local rides or relevant events. This example in the Cow Hollow area of San Francisco features a vintage van as well as selling site-specific Rapha products. © Smith Collection/Gado/Getty Images

One of the earliest pop-ups was by Nike at the 1996 Atlanta Olympics where they transformed a car park on the edge of the Olympic site.

Brands have used and adapted this philosophy to engage customers in a cost-effective manner as the outlay in terms of rental and fit-out costs is relatively minimal and the format allows for onsite flexibility to monitor and gauge consumer reactions.

Another example of this is IKEA's Dining Club which we saw in Chapter 1 (pg. 19). This space was more focussed towards offering a specific experience, providing a place where visitors could have dinner or a party.

Brand experiences and collaborations

In order for customers to feel the brand, collaborations with artists and designers of different types are a way of promoting the brand in particular circles, therefore enhancing its attraction. In recent years, we have seen a rise in celebrities endorsing products with their name, which in turn is their brand, to raise the status of a product type and to give the consumer the opportunity to, in some small way, become them. The sale of perfume is a good example of this.

Whether the brand is a celebrity endorsement, collaboration between the arts and brand or the sponsorship of an event, the outcome impacts on the interior space for its duration. The space in some cases becomes a one-off event in itself or a temporary interior installation becomes the centre point of the store or gallery. This communicates an air of exclusivity to consumers who are quick enough and in the know, enabling them to buy into the brand for a limited period or to experience the brand as an installation rather than a place to shop.

**Figure 2.27 SONY PLAYSTATION®
EVENT Various locations DESIGNER,
CHECKLAND KINDLEYSIDES, 2007** To
celebrate PlayStation's six-month season of
arts collaborations with the Baltic, English
National Opera and British Film Institute, an
iconic interactive installation was designed
and moved to different venues. The mirrored
sculptural form was developed to enhance its
surroundings and reflect the rich visual content
of each venue. © Checkland Kindleysides

**Figure 2.28 WATER LESS
Sculpture DESIGNER, IAN
Mc CHESNEY ARCHITECTS,
2011** This was a collaboration
between Ian McChesney
Architects and Levi's to
promote a new denim that
required less water to wash
it. The sculptural installation
sends a strong visual message
and positions the brand as
innovative and imaginative.
© Glasshopper via Ian
McChesney

Brand Safari

For this exercise you will need to visit a high street or shopping mall, somewhere that has a variety of brands adjacent to each other.

Begin by observing the range of brands available and look for similarities and differences. How are they expressing themselves in terms of simple elements such as colour, graphics and relationship to the street or mall? Are they inviting?

Next, choose two stores that you wish to study further. Ideally they should be different in their approach. Observe and record how they communicate their brand. You should consider the following elements:

- Visual – How do they use graphics, materials and colour to communicate their brand?

- Behaviour – What is your overall impression, how do staff interact, is the shop tidy and well maintained?

- Experience – Record your impressions of the store through diagrams and photos. Do you feel at ease, is the layout legible, is it easy for you to find what you are looking for? What are the other people like in the store?

From this try and describe what you feel the overall personality of the brand is. If it helps, try and think of what it might be if it were a car, a film star or an animal. How do you feel relative to this – are you a customer or potential customer? Try and describe what the target group for the brand is.

Record this for both stores and then list what you think might be the similarities and the differences between the two. You might summarize your findings as in the diagram opposite.

Use this diagram to inform your Brand Safari explorations; it will make a useful template.

Brand 1

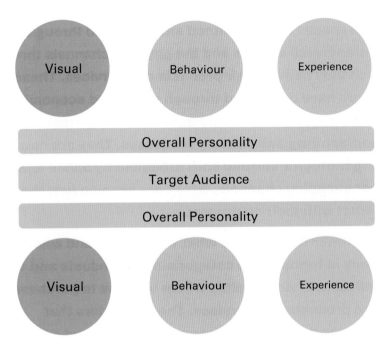

Brand 2

Retail spaces can be defined and identified through different retail sectors and the physical channels through which they deliver their products and services. These sectors have developed through social and economic conditions, politics, history and the development of manufacturing and delivery processes. They are now going through a seismic shift prompted by online and other shopping channels, which are shaping how they interact with their customers.

THIS CHAPTER investigates what we shop for and where we buy in terms of the categorising of products and the physical (and virtual) sites where we seek to purchase those products and services. The key factors that determine how retail environments are shaped and defined is through two main characteristics:

- The sector in which goods and services are categorised

- The channel through which they are delivered

These two factors allow the customer to navigate the range of retail offers and also allow the retailer to focus their offer towards their target audiences.

Increasingly these are becoming more closely linked, particularly in an interconnected environment that is characterized by the current battle between Amazon and Google for a wider slice of customers' spending power. This is delivered through a single channel across a wide range of sectors but strengthens the link between internet and physical brands.

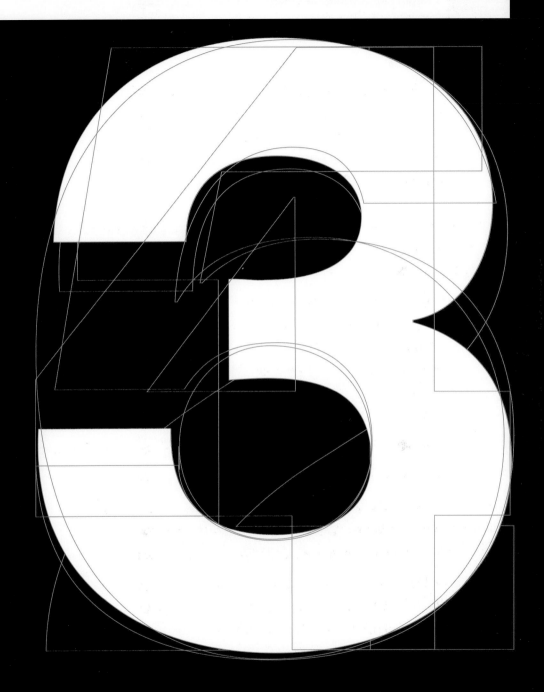

This book is predominantly focused on the physical retail environment but this is increasingly being shaped to provide a platform to support a range of opportunities for purchase and interaction. In this respect there is an increasing convergence of sectors, coupled with cross-sector partnerships and the crossover of tried and tested methods from one sector to another.

In contrast is the increasing popularity of the artisan food market which specializes in a very specific sector delivered through an authentic, personalized and small-scale channel such as an individual shop or small chain.

BEZOS J, CEO, AMAZON

'If you do build a great experience, customers tell each other about that. Word-of-mouth is very powerful.'

Figure 3.1 **AMAZON** From an initial offer of books, it now sells a huge range of products across almost all of the main retail sectors. This includes physical stores and Amazon Dash, a rapid replenishment device used in conjunction with Amazon Fresh, a delivery supermarket. © Bryan Bedder/Getty Images for Amazon Studios

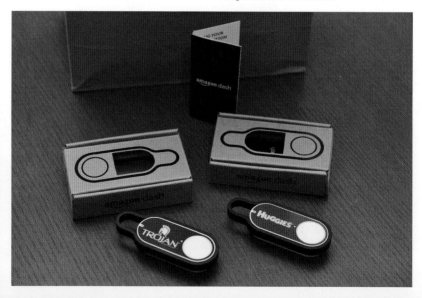

Figure 3.2 ROCKAR Forms links with car companies to sell cars in busy retail locations such as shopping malls in a highly personalised way. © Dalziel & Pow

Figure 3.3 DEVOCION, BROOKLYN Artisan brands are creating authentic experiences; this particular coffee outlet sources the beans and roasts them to produce the freshest coffee possible, with a sister café in the coffee beans' country of origin. © Devocion

The following section will look in more detail at how various sectors have developed and the how they manifest themselves through a variety of channels.

They are defined as follows:

- Food and Beverage – the evolution of the market into supermarket and speciality food stores
- Fashion – clothing, shoes, accessories and beauty products
- Home and Lifestyle – DIY, furniture, fabrics and cookware
- Leisure and Entertainment – sport, technology, travel and finance.

Retail channels

In the retail environment of the future, the relationship between the variety of retail channels will become increasingly important, in particular how this will influence and react with the physical retail environment. However, current research suggests that the new generation of consumers known as Generation Z actually prefer shopping in a physical store.

: **JWT RESEARCH**

'a staggering 67% of the UK's Gen Z would rather shop in a physical store than online.'

Food and Beverage

Fashion

Home and lifestyle

Leisure and Entertainment

Figure 3.4 RETAIL SECTORS: This illustrates the key sectors with their associated channels These sectors each have specific requirements and relationships to their customers and markets. However, they should not be considered as individual silos, as the divisions are increasingly merging, especially in the online and omni channel environment.
© Devocion | Ed Reeves Photography/Virgile and Partners | BDP | b8ta

With increased choice and affluence this sector has become a growth area in recent years with the barriers between food retail and consumption beginning to overlap and lose their segregation. The sector is characterized by a wide range of offers and experiences with a focus on the authentic, and an increasing desire to visualize the food chain through provenance and local supply networks.

Whilst the design language of these retail environments is often repeated from town to town and can at first appear monotonous, this change represents a return to an authentic market approach.

These spaces have derived from cultural influences and worldwide traditions, and have been interpreted into a systematic, functional store environment. For instance, many coffee shops and restaurants reflect European café culture, taking advantage of the warm climate with open façades and exterior seating. Similarly, supermarket product displays are reminiscent of street markets and old market halls, with produce stacked high, and the colours of food and packaging utilized to attract sales. The layout of aisles, too, pushing customers in a particular direction, is set out in a similar way to the market but in a much more regimented manner.

Food markets

From the 1960s forward many traditional market halls changed use or were demolished, as supermarket shopping became the norm. In recent times the market hall has seen a re-emergence and although it has lost its core value, it is now a tourist destination and a place for finding specialist high-quality ingredients, arts and crafts, textiles and fashion.

The layout of the market hall tends to be based on rows of permanent shop accommodations overlooking a central open market space for pitching stands.

Consumers are looking for a stronger connection to products, a local outlet and a return to the market experience. This has brought the markets back into the centre in places such as Rotterdam and London and the growth of Farmers Markets in the US. It has also stimulated supermarket and mass retailers to introduce a market feel to their fresh food at all price points.

Food & Beverage

Food Markets	Supermarkets	Food Courts	Specialty & Artisan

Figure 3.5 **FOOD & BEVERAGE** The main sector channels and their interrelationships.

Figure 3.6
**MORRISONS,
M WORLDWIDE,
2015** This food
display seeks
to replicate the
colour and vigour
of a market; this is
reinforced through
the signage,
display and use of
natural materials
such as timber.
© M Worldwide

Figure 3.7 **SMALL
BATCH, Chalk
Architecture, 2008**
There has been a cultural
shift towards open
façades and exterior
seating, even in cooler
Northern climates.
© Jim Stephenson/
www.clickclickjim.com

Case Study

This modern market hall, recently
completed by MDRDV, creates a vibrant
covered space which seeks to replicate
the original idea of the market within
the community. The development
combines residential units with the
market space, incorporating food and
beverage units.

The space has been designed to allow
the individual stalls to speak to their
customers within an overall design
language.

The overall space is enlivened by a
colourful mural by artists Arno Coenen
and Iris Roskam, which covers the
inside of the arch creating a pop art-like
environment.

Figures 3.8, 3.9 and 3.10 **MARKET HALL
ROTTERDAM, MVRDV, 2015** © MDRDV

Supermarkets

The supermarket experience is now a familiar environment that provides for a range of customers' needs. The relationship between supermarkets and markets is evident in the reason for their existence and the translation of product display, and this relationship is becoming stronger. What the supermarket does, however, is enable the maintenance of the current pace of living with its convenience in an environment that is contemporary and fulfilling of aspirations.

Fierce competition in this market in recent years has led to some innovative approaches based on price, quality and experience across all price points. One significant change is the end of large scale 'single weekly' shopping to much more focussed purchases, perhaps supplemented by online order and delivery of essential items. The quality of produce and presentation has become a key area providing more of a market feel, particularly with fresh produce, but this has also spread to include in-store bakeries, coffee shops and recipe ideas.

Modern shoppers are also keen to know what we are eating and where the produce is from and this has led to an individual approach, particularly with fresh food, reflecting back to a market style approach.

Food courts and shared eating spaces

Food courts initially developed from the Hawkers Markets of Southeast Asia where the idea of choosing foods from a variety of offers in a shared seating environment is a unique culinary experience. They have proved extremely popular and have evolved into an integral part of the shopping centre experience to increase the richness of the customer experience and provide a more attractive destination.

The idea of shared or refectory style eating is not new, originating in universities and monasteries, but it has gained traction as we have become more relaxed about communal eating.

Increasingly the purchase and consumption of food is beginning to integrate and merge, becoming an integral part of the shopping and leisure experience. This is noticeable both in the mall experience but also in city shopping environments with the emergence of specialist food areas adjacent to major retailing streets.

Specialty and artisan outlets

These stores began to crop up in affluent neighbourhoods a few years ago, largely as a response to the bland environment of larger food retailers but also through an increasing interest in the quality and provenance of what we eat. There is also a strong sense of identity with the local community and a return to the age of individuality and craft in the retail experience.

They are typically run by small groups of individuals emphasizing small-scale, high-quality production with a passion for what they do. Finance has become easier in recent years through crowdfunding sites.

Figure 3.11 BFRESH, BOSTON, Blink, 2015 The displays in this supermarket reflect that of an artisan bakery with attention to detail and product displays.
© www.blink.se

Figure 3.12 ALBERT HEIJN, Blink, 2015 The industrial feel and scale of the spaces give the feeling of a market hall.
© www.blink.se

Figure 3.13 NEWTON CIRCUS, SINGAPORE The idea of choosing food from a variety of offers and consuming it in a communal environment originated in Hawkers Markets. This is one of the largest and oldest in Singapore. © Peter Charlesworth/LightRocket via Getty Images

Figure 3.14 NOTCUTTS, DALZIEL & POW 2016 This food area in a garden centre uses appropriate imagery coupled with tempting food displays and a festival atmosphere to create a memorable eating experience. © Dalziel & Pow

They are characterized by an individual approach to the making and serving of the produce together with a transparency that allows the customer to feel part of and sometimes engaged in the experience. The interior environment is frequently crafted to reflect the individual offer of the store and their owners. In recent years these have also started to be introduced into food areas in shopping centres such that customers can buy as well as consume food in these areas.

Figure 3.15 **T2, LONDON: Landini Associates, 2014**
Part of the attraction of this specialty tea shop is the theatre of both the space and the delivery of the product. It produces an authentic setting for the appreciation of the speciality teas served.
© Landini Associates
landiniassociates.com

Fashion has an important influence on the retail sector. Firstly, the interior space is designed to reflect current trends in colour, material and graphics. Secondly, the sector is driven by the huge consumer boom in the fashion industry, which covers the sales of clothing, accessories and shoes as well as beauty products.

Fashion is one of the key sectors which has established a strong online presence frequently dovetailing with a successful physical presence to drive sales through multiple channels. This has spawned a number of strong online platforms such as Net a Porter and Asos offering a curated service, keen prices and delivery within hours. This has driven fashion stores to offer unique experiences to their customers and allows brands to speak to their customers in more relevant and meaningful ways.

As the world of fashion is ever changing, fashion stores demand interiors that will appeal to the appropriate market. Fashion retail can be broadly broken down into three areas: premium fashion labels, where innovative, cutting-edge fashions and retail spaces lead the way for their counterparts; boutiques, where the interior space is unique and styled to suit the needs of the individual; and the mass-consumed commercial fashion empire, where fashions and interiors are fast-paced, exciting and sometimes controversial.

This has enabled the design of the retail environment to be able to speak directly to the customer about their brand and its relevance to them, which might manifest itself in customization, exclusivity, aspiration or value. The unique aspect of fashion in terms of its relationship to the physical form provides a strong platform for engagement with the customer, which allows the designer to create engaging experiences to drive desire.

: **ROGER WADE, BOXPARK**

'Retail is about emotions. Not seeing, feeling and interacting with merchandise makes buying online feel like watching fireworks on TV.'

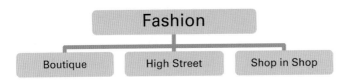

Fashion

Boutique   High Street   Shop in Shop

Figure 3.16 SECTOR DIAGRAM Some of the key fashion channels are outlined here, others have been dealt with previously.

Figure 3.17 STELLA MCCARTNEY 2016 GB OLYMPIC APPAREL Fashion designers and brands are increasingly working outside of their key sectors. © Handout via Getty Images

The fashion interior has become an important method of making customers aware of the aspirations of the brand at all price points. This is highlighted by examples such as the Primark flagship stores in New York and Madrid which use elements from high-end retailers and sports brands such as Nike to create an aspirational environment for value products. In areas of sports sponsorship we are seeing retailers such as Uniglo sponsoring tennis stars such as Novak Djokovic.

This sector has seen significant growth in recent years with the emergence of a new generation of designers such as Stella McCartney and Marc Jacobs bridging couture fashion with diffusion ranges and a strong range of accessories. This allows a wide audience to buy into the brand at a variety of price points.

The fashion house

The fashion house is a term that is used to describe an exclusive fashion label, which has a designer or collection of designers working under its name. The premium fashion interior has become the most influential and creative of retail spaces and has fuelled a fertile fusion of fashion and architectural design. The large fashion houses often implement their major brand stores in London, Paris, Milan and New York, as these are considered the most prestigious fashion capitals of the world.

The relationship between the fashion designer and architect allows the fashion designer to gain a strong, unique identity that the architect is able to realize in a quick timeframe.

These stores are frequently a mixture of brand experience and a testing ground for new ranges or approaches. They frequently host exhibitions or live performances to create a continuing dialogue between the brand and customer.

These continue to develop and some recent examples include extensions such as the 'Brand Embassies' of Galeria Melissa in New York, which features amongst other things a kinetic display of twenty-one acrylic boxes that constantly move and change.

Boutique retail

The boutique is an edited collection of custom-made or one-off speciality pieces – in contrast to the more prominent brand stores in the premium market place. The interiors are small, considered and individually designed to suit the image of the clothing and accessories.

There are some interesting variations on this which explore the idea of curating a select range of brands. A noteworthy early example of this is the Dover Street Market by Rei Kawakubo, the creator of Comme des Garçons. This flexible space not only showcases the brand but also encourages crossovers with other brands and is characterized by innovative displays and artworks that are constantly changing.

Figure 3.18 and 3.19 **GALERIA MELISSA** Brazilian fashion brand Melissa uses their network of stores as a series of individual experiences which include a high level of Audio Visual integration. These have a strong link with their social media platforms.
© Echochamber

High street

This environment has changed radically over the past few years where it used to be dominated by chain stores with numerous identical shops in major towns and cities with the same offer available in every high street. These shops often take reference from premium fashion brands in terms of both clothing collections and interiors, and customers expect a high level of finish despite the price point.

This is a heavily competitive market and designers will be working with a range of other professionals from marketing, logistics, brand and possibly even the brand's in-house design team.

Figure 3.20 **OKI-NI BOUTIQUE London, UK DESIGNER, 6A ARCHITECTS DATE, 2002** Oki-Ni sells exclusive custom-made clothes from design houses such as Evisu, Levi's and Adidas. The interior scheme of its London store is based on an oak 'tray' that acts like a stage, with piles of felt layered to create platforms for product display. Oki-Ni has offered the fashion market a fresh relationship between consumer and product. Limited edition clothes by global and independent brands are available exclusively online from Oki-Ni. 6a architects won the commission to design the flagship store on Savile Row with an installation-based concept that emphasizes the tactile and social opportunities of clothes shopping. Low piles of felt replace the traditional arrangement of shelving, rails and furniture, and define Oki-Ni's physical landscape; the generous felt surfaces are both display and furniture. This departure from the established conventions of retail design creates a place where resting and socializing play a critical part in the discovery of new products. © David Grandorge courtesy of 6a architects

Figure 3.21 **DOVER STREET MARKET** A flexible space creates the setting for a variety of fashion brands which is constantly revolving, always engaging and ever changing; the appeal is further enhanced by one-off exhibitions and events. © David M. Benett/ Getty

Figure 3.22 and 3.23 TOPSHOP New York, USA DESIGNER,DALZIEL AND POW,
2009 Topshop is one of the UK's leading commercial fashion retailers. The launch of their New
York flagship store in 2009 marked the transition to global brand. Replicating many of the design
features found in UK stores, Dalziel and Pow have created a bold and confident statement and have
successfully carried the brand across to the US market. © Dalziel & Pow

Shop in shop

Sometimes also referred to as 'concessions' these are designated areas, usually within a department store, which are fitted out to the retailer's concept and generally include paypoints and changing rooms, although these are sometimes provided as a shared resource. They generally have a relatively short lifespan and in this respect they have some similarities to an exhibition although this does not preclude the use of quality materials and high design values.

Figure 3.24 and 3.25 WONDER ROOM, SELFRIDGES London, KLEIN DYTHAM ARCHITECTURE, 2007 The creation of an architectural series of rooms within the overall store format creates an upmarket, exclusive feel that reflects the brands it represents.

The idea of a curated area has been taken further by department stores such as Selfridges in the UK and Barney's in the US to create strongly themed areas such as the 'Wonder Room' and 'Fragrance Lab' which provide a curated and sensory experience of luxury.

© View Pictures/UIG via Getty Images

Consumer culture thrived in America in the 1950s and the home featured predominantly in the role of the suburban housewife; kitchen gadgets and appliances became must-have items.

In the UK, the Festival of Britain, held in 1951, was a celebration of Britain's past, present and future and saw the launch of the new 'Contemporary Style', which was derived from both American design and European Modernism, but was embedded with British traditions. Furniture could be bought from only a small number of high street retailers. Interior decoration and home DIY were becoming Britain's post-war pre-occupation, and therefore the need for paint, wallpaper, flooring and furniture had a positive impact on the retailing industry.

In the 2000s the idea of the home became a focus for people's spending, and the idea of 'lifestyle' was promoted in journals and TV programmes; the cycle of renovation of people's homes became ever shorter. This has stimulated a boom in this sector from world-wide mass market retailers such as IKEA through to lifestyle retailers such as The Line

and Fritz Hansen and has made this the widest area of retail activity.

This has further developed through the increase in entertaining at home fuelled by celebrity chef TV programmes, increasing access to home entertainment and the ideal of the Scandinavian 'hygge' lifestyle.

Lifestyle and consumption

The idea of lifestyle was first introduced in the early 1960s when Terence Conran launched his first furniture showroom, Habitat, in London. Conran's aim was to introduce his commercial furniture range to the domestic market and was a reaction to the lack of good, affordable furniture shops in the UK at that time. Influenced by the markets and shops of France and Northern Italy, the store became very successful in bringing a diverse range of inexpensive lifestyle products to the high street. Some of the cookware products had never been seen on the British market before. The pots, pans and other cookware items were stacked high like on the European market stalls, and this has now become recognisable as the Habitat retail concept.

Figure 3.26 **HOME & LIFESTYLE CHANNELS** This illustrates the main areas of activity but there are many subdivisions which will be referred to in the text.

Figure 3.27 **HABITAT IN THE 1960s** The interior of one of the first Habitat stores in the UK. © Evening Standard/Getty Images

Figure 3.28 **Muji Store MUJI TODAY** The simplicity of the 'no brand' concept has had a tremendous influence on retail design. © View Pictures/UIG via Getty Images

In 1974, Habitat launched its first Basics range – a collection of 100 home products at very low prices. The range was a huge success and enabled the company to attract a new clientele as well as ride out the recession. When the idea was re-launched in 1982, Habitat was franchised in Japan. The Japanese loved the Basics idea and asked for permission to launch the concept under a different name. The concept store Muji was born and is now a leading retailer of 'no-brand' products that are simply packaged and sold cheaply with the emphasis on recycling and 'no-waste'.

TERENCE CONRAN

'. . . a better style of life should be more widely available. Habitat showed that you need to follow the same philosophy right through from drawing board, via manufacturing, to the retail shop floor. . . . This is what Habitat achieved in the 1960s. . . .'

IKEA and peak stuff

The biggest innovation in furniture design of the late 1940s was flatpack furniture by the Swedish designer, Gillis Lundgren. IKEA later went on to develop their store concept around this idea and opened the first store in Sweden in 1958. The idea was to promote cheap, mass-produced furniture and homeware that was easily accessible. The flatpack furniture is easy to store and assemble, thus affecting the sale price and the design of the showroom. The IKEA store as we know it consists of a showroom, marketplace and warehouse. The idea of the layout is that the customer walks a particular long route so that they view all of the products and room sets for inspiration, and note down the reference of the furniture they wish to buy. This spatial structure was new to retailing and promoted mass consumerism and accessibility.

In 2016 the company's Head of Sustainability Steve Howard declared that we had reached 'peak curtains'.

Although IKEA was relating this to the company's move towards more circular environmental policies it can also be seen as a move towards retailing becoming as much about creating experiences as with selling things. We will see later that this philosophy tiers through the whole of this sector and its channels.

Retail malls

Shopping centres or malls were pioneered in America during the 1950s. The malls were generally built on the outskirts of the cities and had plenty of parking space and service areas for suitable access.

The rapid expansion of the mall, particularly in America, caused many town centres to become virtual ghost towns but this has been reversed in the last few years such that the mall has had to reinvent and broaden its offer.

In addition new tenant mixes have become more varied with cinemas, food and entertainment as well as technology retailers such as Apple and the likes of Tesla in the US and Rockar in Europe successfully selling cars within a mall environment.

Since the mid-1980s the mall has moved to become a destination with a mixture of shopping, entertainment and food offers. These have become increasing more sophisticated, offering a more seamless mixture of retailing, food and entertainment; it is becoming increasingly common for peoples prime reason to visit a shopping mall to be socially related rather than an opportunity to purchase goods.

> : **STEVE HOWARD: HEAD OF SUSTAINABILITY IKEA**
>
> 'If we look on a global basis, in the west we have probably hit peak stuff. . . . peak home furnishings.'

Figure 3.29 **WESTGATE CENTRE, OXFORD** This centre combines high end retail with experiences such as a circus performance.
© John Phillips/Getty Images for Westgate Oxford

FUNG GLOBAL RETAIL & TECHNOLOGY

'The mall is not dead. It is, however evolving at a pivotal time in the context of a changing retail landscape and shifting consumer demand. The new mall is an exciting, hybrid format encompassing retail, entertainment, food outlets, housing, education and even medical facilities in some cases.'

Although the majority of mall designers and developers are international in their spread of work there has been a focus towards local relevance, particularly in the regional shopping habits of customers and the context of the mall. Increasingly malls are less individual destinations and tend to form clusters around entertainment, hotels and sometimes galleries and cultural attractions such as The Shoppes at Marina Bay in Singapore.

Figure 3.30, 3.31 and 3.32 ZLOTE TARASY Warsaw, Poland DESIGNER, THE JERDE PARTNERSHIP INC., 2007 Shopping centres can bring new life to urban areas. Zlote Tarasy, a multi-level, mixed-use project located in central Warsaw, serves as a connection to the city and creates a model for further urban redevelopment in the area. The design takes its inspiration from Warsaw's historic urban parks, with an undulating glass roof, organized terraces and generous open spaces.
© Marcin Czajkowski courtesy of the Jerde Partnership

Integrated design

The design and build of a shopping centre is a good example of how architects, landscape designers and interior designers work together. The architect is responsible for the building scheme and working out the general circulation and division of space; the landscape designer specializes in planting in the malls and outdoor spaces, whilst the interior designer, often specializing in retail design, brings the building to life with theatre, lighting, materials, and public spaces with seating and graphics. The role of the interior designer can also extend to the fit-out of the retail units.

The experience of shopping in a mall begins in the car park or associated transport hub, which is very accessible and commonly integrated into the building. Signage and graphics play a major role in aiding navigation and these tend to be prominent at the earliest touchpoints. Maps and hanging banners are clearly visible and define the brand of the centre. Some malls are configured in straight rows whilst others are more meandering or have a circular navigation. Many are set out over several floors with escalators and lifts connecting the spaces. The walkways are very wide and have planting and seating to break up the space. The shopfronts face the walkways and sometimes pop out to make them more visible.

The shopping centre generally comprises a number of different-sized shop units with 'anchor' stores at key points or nodes. The 'anchor' stores are typically well-known department stores that take up a large area of the shopping centre and act as a magnet to draw customers through the mall – sometimes the anchor is a cinema or bowling alley. The integration of food offers can either be a central feature such as a food court or are distributed throughout the mall to create a range of opportunities to rest and refresh. This all adds to the experience of a day out. Toilets, banking facilities and cafés appear at regular intervals. Shopping centres are accessible for families and sometimes have crèche facilities, as well as baby changing in the toilets and high chairs in the food halls and cafés.

Retail units

Retail units in a shopping centre are fairly straightforward to fit out without having to adjust the architectural elements of the space. Unless the centre is new, an old scheme may have to be ripped out first, but this is usually non-structural. They are purpose built and always provide a rear door for deliveries and services, adequate space for storage adjacent to the delivery door, a discreetly positioned soil vent pipe connection for staff facilities, accessible electric hook-up and a position on the roof of the building or outside wall for air conditioning. The design of the unit has to be approved by the shopping centre management team and must adhere to the design guidelines of the centre, as well as usual building regulations. The shopfront design is the most contentious part of the design package, as it must work alongside the other traders without obscuring the view of its neighbours, and must sometimes include generic architectural details that are apparent throughout the malls. There is often very little natural light into the retail units, the only source being from the covered mall. Therefore, artificial lighting plays an important role in the whole retail scheme.

Figure 3.33
TENANT GUIDELINES
An example of the types of guidelines that are part of the developer's package that a designer will have to work within.
© BDP

spine side
Ideas & Inspiration
Tenant fitted storefronts for an unique retail experience

Focus on Entrance
· Glazed or partially solid
· Use a recess to accentuate entrance - max 1.5m (5 ft) depth
· Robust materials

Refined Branding Opportunity
· Integrated into storefront architecture
· Individual Lettering
· Internally illuminated

Animate Full Height
· Illumination
· Treatment to wall
· Treatment to lower glazing area

Dark Grey Metal Pilaster

Dia. F1

Strong Brand Presence
· Repeat signature finishes from exterior to interior
· Focus on Display
· Quality materials & details throughout

Inset Pedimat
· Required for all retail units
· Minimum 1 m (3.3 ft.) up to 3m (10 ft.) in walking direction depth

Framed Storefront
· Framed Glazing
· Framed Display
· Framed Door

Landlord Blade Signage
· For tenant logo display
· Opaque white logos only
· See Standards section for more details

Figure 3.34 Typical Tenant Unit Retail units in a retail mall are generally prepared to a shell finish for fitting out by the tenant. Generally services will be provided together with a prepared opening for the shopfront. © Stephen Anderson

Out-of-town retail and outlet centres

Out-of-town shopping extends far beyond the realms of the shopping centre. The landscape of many countries is scattered with large warehouse-type buildings that contain endless amounts of merchandise. The advantage of out-of-town shopping is in enabling accessibility. Towns and cities are often limited in parking space and have heavy traffic congestion.

The out-of-town experience has an abundance of parking and is often situated near major roads. The downside, however, is the effect these buildings have on the countryside and the ever-decreasing areas of natural beauty. There are traders that naturally fit into out-of-town retail spaces, which can be broken down into the categories of outlet centres or villages, retail parks, megacentres and hypermarkets.

The retail outlet or village is designed around the idea of a shopping mall, and can be open to the elements or under a covered mall. The village will include a food court and the usual public conveniences alongside large retail units. The units are warehouse-like and often constructed from brick and steel with full-height glazed shopfronts.

Initially conceived as a way of disposing of unprofitable or sample lines these have now become an important area of retail design. They have become destinations in their own right allowing brands to maintain their premium whilst offering goods at a lower price point. Stores tend to be a more basic version of mall and high street formats but still maintain a strong sense of the brand experience.

The new wave of outlet stores delivers a complete brand experience and, despite the discounted prices, they are increasingly becoming an important part of the retail language and brand portfolio.

Figure 3.35 **WOODBURY COMMON, NY** Many outlet centres adopt a smaller scale approach and attempt to create a 'village' atmosphere. © Emile Wamsteker/Bloomberg via Getty Images

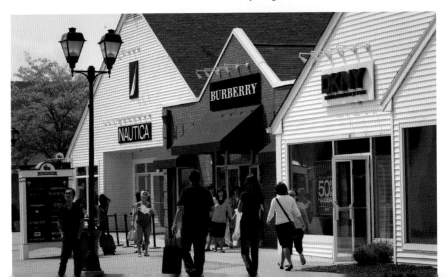

N.K. SCOTT

'The phenomenon of the out-of-town shopping centre, the out-of-town business park, leisure centre, university or any other human activity is singular to our age. The reason is simple and a consequence of the invention of the internal combustion engine.'

Retail parks and showrooms

For some retailers, the out-of-town location is the ideal solution for their product type. Large items such as furniture and DIY paraphernalia, cars, white goods, outdoor and gardening equipment all benefit from having easy access in terms of deliveries and storage. The warehouse-like spaces work well for displaying large items and creating lifestyle spaces such as room sets, which help the customer buy into the product. The units also work well as showrooms for cars due to the open plan nature of the space and large frontages for manoeuvring stock.

New mall formats

As the mall format continues to evolve there has been a move towards shorter leases and more tenant flexibility, especially from young start-up retailers. Coupled with the use of urban infill sites has led to some innovative formats.

Boxpark is the world's first pop-up mall – fusing the concepts of the modern street food market and placing local and global brands side by side, to create a unique shopping and dining destination.

Figure 3.36 PON CATERPILLAR SHOWROOM Leude, Netherlands DESIGNER, QUA, 2003 This project saw the rebranding of CAT, establishing the values, and applying them to the architecture and interior of a completely new building. The building includes a CAT shop as well as the only showroom for Caterpillar bulldozers in the world. © QuA Associates

Opened in 2011, Boxpark, initially in London's Shoreditch, is constructed entirely out of refitted shipping containers. Boxpark offers a unique proposition in being able to offer affordable and flexible conditions for lifestyle brands, cafes, restaurants and galleries to trade and succeed.

Department stores

The popularity of shopping as a leisure activity took off in the nineteenth century with the rise of a British phenomenon: the department store. For the first time, huge arrays of products were available under one roof.

The interior of the department store is controlled by an in-house team of designers whose job it is to dress window displays, design the layout of the store and its concessions, implement signage and other graphics, and maintain a cohesive scheme throughout the store.

Individual stores – my home

One of the strongest trends in the area of home and lifestyle has been to identify the interior with a particular space or place to define and enhance the narrative. This may range from ideas of 'home' and particularly the Scandinavian concept of 'hygge', to ideas of authentic experiences such as Adidas and the idea of the 'locker room'.

> **PAULA NICKOLDS: CEO JOHN LEWIS**
>
> 'We're modernising to reflect society. Consumers see retail as a leisure day out. We want to provide that.'

Figure 3.37 BOXPARK, SHOREDITCH This vibrant mix of retail, food and entertainment draws wide range of emerging retailers. The flexibility allows the mix to be constantly edited and reconfigured. © Alex Segre

Figure 3.38 HARVEY NICHOLS STORE Istanbul, Turkey DESIGNER FOUR IV, 2006 This three-floor, 86,000-square-foot store, complete with food market and a 100-cover restaurant, showcases the very best in Western contemporary retailing, complemented by rich swatches of local material and the traditional skills of Turkish craftsmen. The design details are an exercise in exuberance. The fascia entrance is in polished black stone and gold embossing, the ground floor is virtually crystalline, and the lingerie area features a central chandelier of glass polished butterflies and high-pile carpet. Gilt, a 100-cover restaurant, sits atop the Harvey Nichols store. Serving international food in an environment featuring fine traditional handiwork, the restaurant itself is a destination in its own right. © James Winspear courtesy of Four IV

Figure 3.39 and 3.40 HARVEY NICHOLS Birmingham, UK DESIGNER, VIRGILE & PARTNERS, 2015 Here the designer has created a free-flow store layout with a range of materials, contrasting rough and smooth surfaces. The subtle branding reinforces the iconic nature of the brand and creates a significant departure from the typical 'shop within shop' approach taken by many department stores. © Ed Reeves Photography/Virgile and Partners

Figure 3.41 **FRITZ HANSEN REPUBLIC, LONDON BDP, 2011** This showroom for a leading Scandinavian furniture brand incorporates a full kitchen to welcome visitors, serving coffee in the morning and hosting frequent evening events. © BDP

The concept of the 'retail apartment' was first started by Moss in New York in 1994 whereby the experience was shaped around the idea of a zoned apartment where everything was for sale. This allows for personalization and curation but also promotes the exclusivity of individual and unique pieces and the ability for visitors to view products in a domestic scale context.

This has been developed in some cases such as The Line in Los Angeles where the entire retail space was once actually someone's apartment.

Figure 3.42 **The Line Apartment, Los Angeles** THE LINE APARTMENT, LA; DESIGNER, THE LINE, 2015 The idea of creating a home space is nothing new but The Line takes it to another level. Designed in-house, this concept is a quiet oasis of curated design on Melrose Avenue, Los Angeles. Creating an inspiring series of rooms, objects and products are arranged in a lifestyle setting. © the Line

Case Study

Figures 3.43, 3.44 and 3.45 **Space Ninety 8, Brooklyn SPACE NINETY 8, Brooklyn, in-house design** This concept, developed by Urban Outfitters, seeks to create a variety of experiences within the envelope of the store which has a flexible format. Set over four floors, the ever-changing layout can incorporate brand focus displays as well as events and lifestyle and beauty offers. The offer's range includes gourmet restaurant as well as brand focus areas and a market place specializing in crafted items.

They achieve this by sometimes borrowing techniques from exhibition design, particularly in the way that products are arranged to create 'retail stories' around a specific theme or product range.

The store layout allows for a range of focal elements within the store which may be brand, lifestyle or category focussed; this provides both interest and a freshness to every visit. This example replicates a California surfer's garage lounge.
© Echochamber

The emergence of retail as a leisure activity has allowed it to meaningfully expand into areas where it traditionally does not have a strong presence, particularly in the areas of museums and art galleries where retail has become a central part of both the experience and an income generator.

Curatorial retail

In some respects this can be seen as a direct response to the range of products available and the constant improvement and innovation in product areas, particularly in technical and electrical.

We can probably also draw comparisons with the personal shopper service provided by many high end fashion and department stores whereby purchases are curated towards the customer's tastes. In many respects this is like the act of exhibition curating; it also follows through to the methods of display and layout of the stores with high levels of interactivity with the product and comparative information.

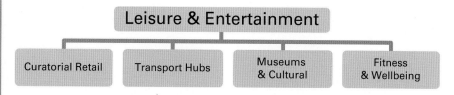

Figure 3.46 **LEISURE AND ENTERTAINMENT** Key sites and channels.

Figures 3.47 and 3.48 THE b8ta STORE, PALO ALTO: IN-HOUSE DESIGN 2015 This store allows customers to interact and discover a wide range of products; it's a totally immersive experience for those wanting to discover and try what's new in technology.

The store encourages customer interaction and makes sure that the newest technology gadgets are always in the store immediately after release and provides trusted recommendations in what can be a confusing marketplace.

The store allows brands to manage their messaging, pricing, and imagery as well as providing information through live insights into capture rates, dwell times and engagement.
© b8ta

Transport hubs

Convenience retail has always been sited in transport hubs such as railway stations much as duty free shops have proliferated in airports. However, as tax regimes have merged and normalized the direct discount, advantages of airport shopping have diminished and made way for lifestyle and particularly luxury brands to create what in some cases resembles a small shopping mall.

Museums and cultural institutions

In recent years museums have moved from stuffy institutions to strong brands and cultural institutions such as MOMA in New York and Tate Modern in London are international brands with significant visitor numbers. Design has played a great part in this from the architecture of the buildings through the exhibits and the retail and food offers.

As well as the accessibility and spectacle of the exhibitions, retail has grown strongly in these areas as visitors want to take away a memory of their experience. This has grown to the extent where blockbuster exhibitions will have their own dedicated retail outlet.

: **RASSHIED DIN**

'Airports have. . . the advantage of knowing who its customers are and when they will be passing through its doors; it is also in the almost unique position of knowing its customers' sex, age and nationality from air-ticket sales, passport information and flight destinations.'

Figure 3.49 SCHIPHOL AIRPORT, Amsterdam, VIRGILE + PARTNERS, 2004 This dramatic intervention of forms into the normally bland airport environment both attracts and creates a destination, breaking the mould to define a series of spaces for shopping, eating and relaxing.
Within the main forms there is a variety of offers from Duty Free goods to food and the Cone Bar.
© Virgile and Partners

Figure 3.50 **MOMA Design Store THE DESIGN STORE, MOMA, NY, Lumsden Design 2016** This project uses a panelled maple wall to provide warmth and sophistication with objects clearly displayed as if in an exhibition. This interior would not look out of place in a boutique or department store. © Martin Seck courtesy of Lumsden Design

Fitness and wellbeing

There has been a marked growth in this area which has been stimulated by increased leisure time/spend and a combination of the rise of male grooming and our desire to take control of our health and look more youthful.

Several areas have characterized this including the extension of sports brands such as Nike wanting to connect with their customers but also shopping centres and department stores providing their customers with a more complete experience.

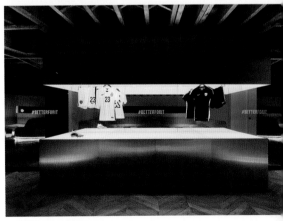

Figures 3.51 and 3.52 **45 Grand, New York 45 GRAND, NEW YORK, NIKE FITNESS STUDIO, RAFAEL DE CÁRDENAS AND ART DIRECTOR JEN BRILL, 2015** This temporary gym, housed in a former auto repair shop, is an expression of Nike's commitment to fitness and features a central naturally lit gym with private lounge areas and a sales area with selected sports clothing.
The ambiance of the space is clean and simple, contrasting the intervention of the exercise areas with the raw quality of the original building. It's primarily a celebrity gym, and membership is invite only to 'influencers'.
© Rafael de Cardenas

Sectors and channels

In this chapter we have looked at the range of sectors and outlets that are commonly experienced in retail design; this exercise provides you with the opportunity to investigate and understand the characteristics that define these.

Observation and research methods

Visit a variety of retail sites which might be a mixture of those detailed in this chapter or even others which you have discovered in your neighbourhood.

During these visits you are encouraged to use a variety of methods of recording what you observe.

Make note of the following:

Sector and Channel

What is the primary sector the site is focused towards?

What type of outlet is it?

Look at how it conforms to the examples in the text and any variations, particularly in terms of layout, brand and format.

Communication

How does the outlet communicate its offer? Is it obvious which sector and customer it is focused towards?

Customers

It is useful to observe which people use the space, how they move through it, preferred pathways, position of key elements, ease of serving, and so on.

Consider the particular social or interest group that might be defined by:

- Age Group
- Culture or Lifestyle
- Shared interests

Look at how these vary between the different sites.

Observe how people use the space; below are some methods you might adopt to do this.

- A Day in the Life

    Look at how people use the space during different periods of the day; lunchtime will be very different from mid-afternoon. This can be mapped on a timeline.

- Camera or Sketch Journal

    Try to record your experiences as a reflective journal, and record what you think works well and where any 'fail points' occur. Don't forget to ask for the owner's permission if you take photographs.

- Observation Log

    Go through the actions of, say, buying a coffee and visualize your findings in a way that communicates the steps and experiences that you went through. Was the process intuitive? How did long did you have to wait? What was working well? What did not?

Recording and communicating

Gather together your research information and consider the following from observations of the sites that you visited:

You should record these using sketches, photographs and artefacts, communicate these clearly through diagrams and perhaps collage. Try to create engaging diagrams of your visits.

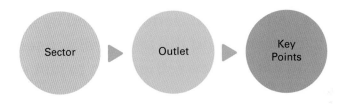

In the modern retail landscape the environment is an essential tool for creating an engaging and memorable experience for the customer realized through every aspect of the store. Increasingly this is a sensory experience shaped by form, space, materials and the use of all senses to create an experience rather than to just sell product.

The retail environment consists of the factors that play on the customer's senses in terms of sight, sound, smell, taste and touch. This transpires through materials and their textures, the use of artificial lighting, the interior climate and the acoustic qualities of the space. The designer has a responsibility to be sensitive to the effects that their design has on the environment and to minimize, where possible, waste and energy use. This, however, is not always under the designer's control, but considering these issues at the forefront of the design process can minimize risk to the environment further down the line.

THIS CHAPTER aims to guide you through the range and selection of the factors that influence the interior environment. It also raises questions surrounding the ecological effects that retail and construction have on the environment and the ways in which they might be addressed.

The world of retail and its connection with consumption is often a controversial subject. Retail is about selling in large quantities, and in order to do this, manufacturing and mass-production is at the heart of the business. This uses vast amounts of materials and the Earth's resources in terms of energy, and creates carbon emissions that are harmful to the environment. Many manufacturers are beginning to address these issues, using materials that are sustainably and locally sourced and processes that are less harmful, but there is still a long way to go before these issues are resolved.

Retail interiors are ripped out and replaced with every new tenant, or changed every five to seven years to keep pace with the market. Also, during the building process, materials are wasted if not used and often end up in landfill rather than being recycled. As designers, part of our role is to consider the materials that are specified in terms of their ability to be reused or to last, or if recycled materials can be used instead. The designer and contractor's team can work together to eliminate waste and consider an alternative use for materials that are left over or substituted.

In terms of energy consumption, electrical and mechanical engineers look carefully at the efficiency of their installations as part of the design process and produce documents that outline to the client the correct way to use the equipment. It is often the misuse of buildings and such equipment that can lead to energy waste.

BREEAM (Building Research Establishment Environmental Assessment Method) is a voluntary measurement rating for green buildings. Now widespread across Europe and the rest of the world, it was initially established in the UK. Its equivalents in other regions include LEED in the USA and Green Star in Australia. In terms of retail, their remit is to carry out assessments on new buildings; major refurbishments, tenant fit-outs; and management and operations assessment on existing buildings. They can look at the general display and sale of goods, food retail and customer service retail. The assessment aims to identify a score that measures the building or fit-out against a set of criteria that will identify any major concerns. Designers now work within the BREEAM guidelines, which in turn help them consider environmental issues.

An analysis of retail and its responsibility to the environment can be broken down into three areas of consideration: the building shell, the interior components and the building's energy consumption.

A sustainable approach

Increasingly retailers and brands are wanting to promote themselves as responsible world citizens and one area that they can demonstrate this is by creating sustainable environments in which to display and sell their products. We have looked at the macro level and it is now worth focussing on the retail interior and particularly the factors that designers can use to minimize our impact on the environment.

This is summarized in the diagram below:

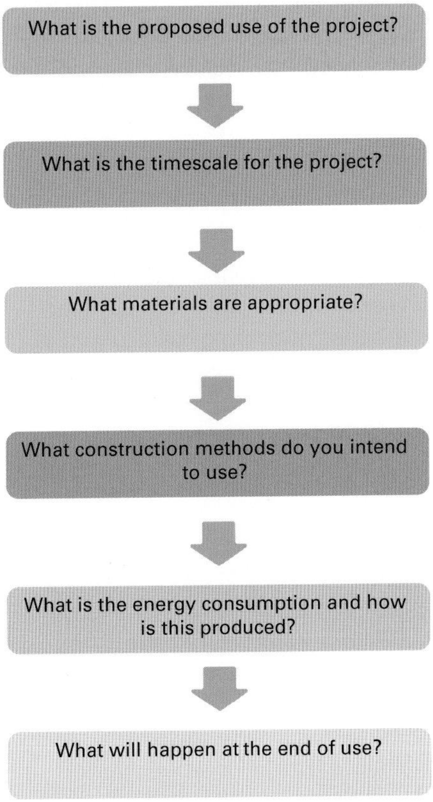

The retail environment is fast moving, driven by a variety of factors which range from ever-changing trends and brand development to degeneration through use or perhaps changing technologies such as lighting and environmental control. Another consideration is the relationship between the retailer and the site where it is likely that they will be renting on a lease from the owner or developer. These will traditionally be for a fixed period but with rent reviews every five years. This allows for flexibility but also needs to be considered in the design, particularly in terms of appropriate materials but also elements such as fixtures and fittings.

What is the proposed use of the project?

⬇

What is the timescale for the project?

⬇

What materials are appropriate?

⬇

What construction methods do you intend to use?

⬇

What is the energy consumption and how is this produced?

⬇

What will happen at the end of use?

Figure 4.1 This diagram provides guidance as to some of the questions that you should be considering at the start of a project. These will help to embed an approach to sustainability at the earliest stages of the project which you should use as a checklist as the project progresses.

The interior shell

The retail interior will always have a context, an existing building, retail unit or existing shop environment; this will shape our initial ideas with regards to the interior and the narrative that we wish to create. We might look at the existing site and recognize features that we wish to retain as part of the interior. Alternatively a blank shop unit in a retail mall provides no such clues and we can begin with a blank canvas.

When considering the interior shell of a building, the key to being sustainable is to think through the interior structure and the choice of materials used. The first consideration should be whether the structure needs to be altered at all; is it useable in its current state? If not, care should be taken so that only minor alterations need to be made. Any structural work, building of walls (including those that are not supporting), the floor finish and ceiling finish is considered part of the interior architecture. Older properties in particular may have seen many structural adjustments in their lifetime so it is important to get the interior shell right structurally to provide an enduring framework for the interior. The key to this is to make the interior structure simple so that fixtures and fittings can be adapted around it. By considering the lifespan of the interior shell, the implemented design can have longevity, reducing the amount of building work over time, and providing a more sustainable response.

The materials used on the floor can also be adopted in this way. A terrazzo floor, for instance, could last more than twenty years if laid properly, as it is both neutral in appearance and durable. Using timber for the flooring also means that reclaimed materials can be reused. This may mean a marked or dented floor but it will again be durable and neutral.

The ceiling plane is an important element of the interior scheme as it houses many of the necessary electrical and mechanical components that make the space function (such as lighting and air conditioning). The architecture of the ceiling plane again can be considered as a fixed element that must be flexible enough in its design to meet the changing interior concept.

In terms of sustainability, the more the existing interior can be kept intact the better; minimizing building work is essential.

> **JUHANI PALLASMAA**
>
> 'We behold, touch, listen and measure the world with our entire bodily existence. . . . We are in constant dialogue and interaction with the environment, to the degree that it is impossible to detach the image of the Self from its spatial and situational existence.'

Figures 4.2 and 4.3 FRITZ HANSEN REPUBLIC SHOWROOM, London, UK Designer, BDP 2011 Here the existing building has a robust aesthetic which is slightly industrial which works well with the Fritz Hansen brand. Internally the result of previous fit-outs have been removed and the existing structure made good to produce a clear, flexible open space; ceilings have been removed and the services are deliberately exposed. © BDP

Creating the interior environment

In the retailing environment there has traditionally been a focus on the visual, primarily to attract the shopper towards products on offer and to define these within specific category areas. This has been enhanced in recent years through the increased integration of audio visual elements and particularly interactive screens. Looking to the future this is no longer enough in a world where consumers can view products over a range of platforms; the modern retail environment needs to be experience led, flexible and responsive. This is achieved through the stimulation of all five senses which is sometimes referred to as a '360° experience'.

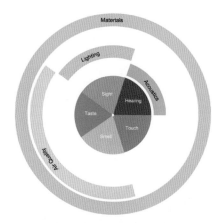

Figure 4.4   How our senses perceive our environment. This diagram illustrates in a simple manner how our senses relate to the key elements of an interior space. This provides us with an indication of how we might use these elements to create a harmonious interior, something that will be looked at in more detail in the following sections. © Stephen Anderson

> **YASUSHI KUSUME, HOW TO CREATE A MEMORABLE BRAND EXPERIENCE, DESIGN COUNCIL**
>
> Just as your perception of someone is formed by every direct or indirect interaction with them, so is your perception of a brand. It is literally everything you have seen and heard - or even felt or smelt or tasted – about it.

Materials

There are literally hundreds of materials available for use in the retail environment. Some are innovative whilst others are commonly found in every space. In terms of sustainability, certain materials can be used to lower the environment's carbon footprint, although it is important to point out that this is still very much a grey area.

Interior designers work predominantly with materials, gauging how they look, feel and enhance the interior environment. The material or sample board is first produced as part of the concept design and is discussed with the client. For every design project the material specification is formulated as part of the design scheme. The specification provides a detailed document of every material, the supplier and cost, as well as its sustainable attributes.

Some materials have structural qualities that are used in the construction stage of the interior; other materials lend themselves to creating the interior look through the fixtures and finishes. In this chapter, the most common materials found in a retail environment are explored.

Material selection is important and not just a factor of aesthetics. For example, there is a diverse range of flooring solutions available. They need to be durable as the amount of traffic moving through the retail interior space is generally high. It is also advantageous to think about the cleaning process and how materials will stand up to polishing machines and other maintenance regimes over time.

There are a number of ways in which we can categorize materials which might help the designer's selection process.

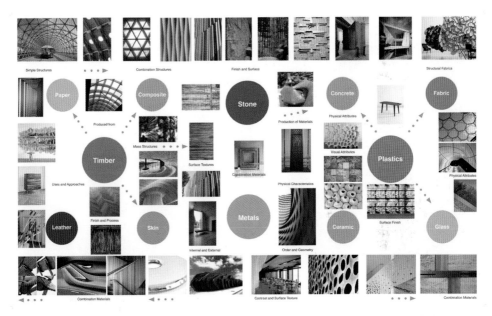

Figure 4.5 Materials can be classified in a variety of ways, for example their physical typology such as timber, metals and ceramics. They can also be classified by their physical characteristics such as hard, soft, reflective or dull. Many material websites will use a variety of classifications and users are able to choose which best suits their search, which can be useful in the early stages of a design. The same generic material can create quite different effects dependant on the processes used and criteria such as the surface treatment and finish, allowing them to be used in different situations.
© Stephen Anderson

Figure 4.6 **K-SPACE CONCEPT STORE London, UK DESIGNER, 6A ARCHITECTS DATE, 2008** Perforated polished stainless steel cladding elicits an ambiguous quality at the meeting point of reflection, transparency and opacity. The object reveals its contents through the perforations and mirrors the surroundings in its surface, creating a constantly changing installation. © David Grandorge courtesy of 6a architects

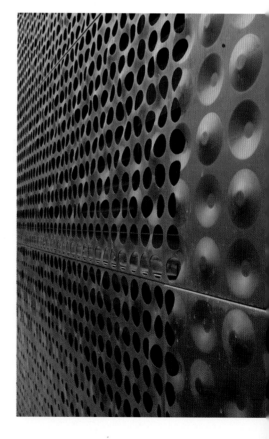

Figure 4.7 **DE YOUNG MUSEUM, San Francisco, Herzog & De Meuron, 2005** Perforated bronze metal is used to create a textural surface as an external skin. The material helps to create a soft edge to the building. © Stephen Anderson

As the material selection process develops it is necessary to go into more detail, particularly with regards to the specific characteristics required for the application of a specific material.

Material Selection Characteristics

Which? Material Choice	Why? Material Characteristics	How? Material Properties	What? On Site Considerations
	Appearance	Finish and Texture Range of Options	Comfort and grip Appropriate to use
Material Choice Which Material?	Durability	Structure Composition	Ages well Resilience to wear
	Flexibilty	State and Process Unique Characteristics	Module and Scale Authentic and Natural
	Sustainability	Source of Supply Disposal and Reuse	Travel Distance Disposal Options

Figure 4.8 In order to help the selection of materials the matrix in Figure 4.8 provides criteria that might be considered in the selection process. It does not include all factors but focusses on the appropriate qualities that might be required – in particular the detail of process, finish and performance in use.

Material decisions are not simply based on a particular material but also aspects such as finish, module and laying pattern. Aspects of cleaning and maintenance should also be considered.

In the following pages there are examples and descriptions of materials typically used in the retail interior, which are illustrated using indicative project references.

Timber

Timber is a versatile material that comes in a range of shades, finishes and textures depending on the timber selected. It can be used as an interior wall cladding, for fixture and furniture construction or as a floor finish. It has warmth and has natural variations, which can add character to a space. Softwoods, mainly pine, are most commonly used for timber-framed fixture carcasses, with an outer skin applied for finishing. Hardwoods such as oak, ash, beech, walnut, cherry and maple are used extensively both as solid timber or thin surface veneers; they are commonly used for flooring.

The use of composites such as MDF and chipboard are used extensively in many retail environments as a substrate for other finishes.

Metals

Stainless steel, aluminium and powder-coated mild steel are commonly used in the retail environment. Steel and aluminium can be used structurally, in a shopfront as a glazing frame, as part of the fixture and furniture design, as system upright posts between wall bays, as a decorative cladding to walls or as part of the signage construction.

The surface finish of metals is particularly important to avoid corrosion, particularly in food environments.

Glass

Glass is incredibly diverse and structurally strong. The retail customer's first experience of the interior and product is generally through the glazed shopfront window. This glass is laminated (layered bonded glass) for strength and safety. Glass is used for shelving, cabinet displays and sometimes screens. Glass can be coloured using a gel, textured or frosted. The use of recycled glass in products such as tiles is becoming particularly popular.

Laminate

Laminates are constructed by layering and fusing kraft or printed papers and resins, with a decorative layer on top, coated in melamine. They are hardwearing and often used as surfaces for counters, wall and door finishes as well as floor finishes mimicking timber. Laminates can be decorative and can be used in innovative ways to create feature walls and displays. They are easy to clean and are durable although once damaged tend to degenerate quickly.

Vinyl, linoleum and rubber

Vinyl flooring comes in sheet or tile form in a variety of colours and finishes. It is used in sheet form mainly in the back of house area of the store and ancillary areas, as it is relatively cheap and hardwearing. Vinyl tiles are

Figure 4.9 **GEORGE JENSEN STORE, JAPAN** Here timber is used in a variety of forms to create a backdrop for the furniture displays. Interest is created not just through the use of different timbers but also through scale and module, the wide flooring boards contrasting with the delicate timber screens.

A simple laminate is used to create a contrast to the form containing ancillary support spaces. © View Pictures/UIG via Getty Images

available in a range of finishes and come in a range of modules to imitate timber or stone. Rubber, like vinyl, comes in sheet and tile formats but can be expensive. It comes in a range of exciting colours and, when sealed, can be water resistant.

Linoleum uses natural materials and has a distinct character and surface texture. It generally comes in sheet format and can be used as a flooring material or a worksurface.

Concrete, terrazzo and quartz

These hard-wearing materials are used predominantly for floor finishes, but sometimes as a wall cladding. Concrete can be polished to give it sheen, coloured with a pigment or moulded to a form of texture, making it very versatile. Concrete, used as a matrix in terrazzo, can be mixed with aggregates such as marble or granite to create a conglomerate, which means that different stones are mixed together. Some conglomerates have quartz added for sparkle. Concrete can be ground down and recycled but this process creates harmful emissions. The manufacture of concrete can also use large amounts of energy.

Natural stone, slate, marble and granite

These are traditional, natural materials that can be mixed with concrete to create a conglomerate, or used on their own for flooring, cladding or surface finish. They are hard wearing and have longevity. Each piece will have its own natural flaws. It is important to mention that some stones such as limestone and sandstone can be very porous and stain easily. Vast amounts of water can be used when quarrying, cutting and polishing the stone; large amounts of energy can also be used in transporting the materials from the quarry to site. These are natural materials which cannot easily be replaced so they should be used appropriately.

Ceramic and porcelain

Composite tiles are made from moulding finely ground ceramic powder under high temperatures and pressure. They are hard wearing and a cost-effective choice. They come in a wide variety of finishes and often mimic the look of real stone. They can be used on the floor, walls or as a mosaic pattern, and are waterproof. The finish can be matt, gloss or a variety of textures.

They come in a wide variety of thicknesses and modules and are increasingly available in large slab formats.

Textiles

Different types of textiles are used widely in retail design, from upholstery and fitting room curtains to carpets. Sometimes, the retail designer will work with an upholsterer to create and customize pieces of furniture. Leather and specialist upholstery fabric are most commonly used. Carpets are sometimes specified for retail environments and can be produced to a specific design or pattern. They come in a variety of finishes, either in man-made or natural fibres. Carpets tend to wear out quickly with heavy traffic and need replacing on a regular basis.

Textiles and carpets are useful for controlling the acoustic quality of a space.

Thin surface finishes

Walls and ceilings can be finished in a wide range of finishes ranging from wallpaper through a variety of paint finishes. Some paints are more environmentally friendly both in terms of their production and emissions; wallpapers can be made from recycled paper and patterned or textured in a range of ways. Wallpaper is once again fashionable and is now widely used both commercially and residentially.

In areas of high use such as display and pay areas the specification of painted surfaces needs to be considered to ensure longevity.

Figure 4.10
CONVERSE FLAGSHIP STORE, NEW YORK, US The combination of concrete, render and ceramic tiles together with a stainless steel ceiling feature create a hard edged urban feel to this flagship store. Retained features such as columns and brickwork reinforce the heritage of the building. © View Pictures/UIG via Getty Images

Figure 4.11 **JOHN RICHMOND STORE, LONDON, UK** This simple palette of materials uses fabric in both the spatial dividers and soft furnishings. The use of glass and a rich ceramic tile add structure and order to the space. © View Pictures/UIG via Getty Images

Evolving materials

Advances in technology and manufacturing techniques have created many new materials useful in retail design. These range from new properties of existing material types such as translucent and fabric concrete to advances in recycled materials and especially plastics.

Many of these materials will perform well in a range of conditions but, as they have not been tested over longer periods of time, caution should be taken when specifying these.

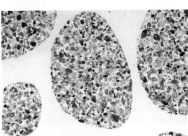

Figures 4.12, 4.13 and 4.14 **SHOE LEVEL DISTRICT, DUBAI MALL, Dubai UK DESIGNER, GILES MILLER STUDIO, 2012** The innovative use of ceramic tiles produces a textural cladding which creates interest and helps to break down the large columns and wall areas. The designers have produced a custom ceramic wall covering featuring tiles arrayed in floral formations in a variety of ceramic finishes. © Giles Miller Studio

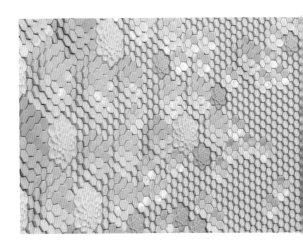

Figures 4.15, 4.16 and 4.17 **THE TIMBERLAND BOOT COMPANY, TRADING SPACE London, UK DESIGNER, CHECKLAND KINDLEYSIDES, 2005** Timberland seeks to engage in a positive and sustainable way with the communities and places located near to the store. As such, the 'spirit' of the store evolves from its context and expresses the company's desire to belong to its locality. For this first site, the design evolved from inventiveness, physically building as little as possible, developing inexpensive and effective solutions through recycling. The building at 1 Fournier Street, London, was previously a banana warehouse and this provided one of the key display concepts for the space. Boots are displayed in clusters hung from the ceilings, resembling bunches of bananas. Box rolling racks unearthed from the basement have been given a new purpose as display tables, and cardboard boxes stacked on specially designed racking have created a stockholding wall at the rear of the store.
© Checkland Kindleysides

Material branding/identity

There is a strong link developing between the emotional characteristics of materials and the brand experience, and many brands have worked to develop this into a clear language of their identity.

Apple in particular has developed a language of elements in their stores, particularly through the use of a dramatic glass staircase. Although there is a variation through each store there is a common language which communicates the core values of transparency and product innovation.

Figure 4.18 **APPLE STORE, San Francisco 2010** The attention to detail and quality of materials in an Apple store is a reflection of the quality and innovation inherent in its products.
© Stephen Anderson

Figure 4.19 **NORTH FACE, Stanford, US, Designer Green Room 2016** Here timber is used in its natural state as a statement both within the store to signify the service desk as well as to reinforce the brands links with nature and the outdoor lifestyle.
© Green Room

Lighting is an important tool in the design of retail spaces. The key design considerations are the balance of artificial light throughout the store and that of natural light which enters though the façade and other controlled points such as windows and skylights.

The retail environment is lit predominantly artificially; natural daylight is evident through the façade but does not always reach into the depth of the store. In addition natural daylight changes throughout the day in terms of its direction and intensity and is affected by the seasons. Artificial lighting is not subject to these changing conditions and can be controlled more accurately. Lighting is used to entice the customer into the store and is used to navigate the customer journey and the display of products.

Artificial lighting has improved significantly since the light bulb was designed and most people are now conscious of the impact that it has on energy consumption (lighting currently accounts for some 40 per cent of energy consumption of non-residential buildings). New lamp technology has given lighting energy-saving efficiency, particularly LEDs, new CDM-T lamps and fluorescent fittings which are now in widespread use.

The brightness of artificial lighting is measured in Lux which is measured at specific points such as the floor or product displays. Retail spaces are known for using high levels of Lux, so in recent years research has been conducted to find out the range in which the human eye perceives differences in light levels. In doing this, retailers have lowered the Lux levels without affecting the overall brightness of the interior. For example, the window display, which used to be 1000 Lux, is the brightest element of the store; this has now changed to 750 Lux following these studies, thus decreasing its environmental impact. In addition, greater importance is now given to focussing lighting on displays rather than a general level and also highlighting elements within the store to provide a depth of visual field.

The retail designer works closely with a lighting designer to create the desired effect for the branded interior. A reflected ceiling plan is drawn to indicate the positioning of light fittings in relation to the displays, products and services. This drawing is really important in terms of setting out the interior space and will contain a key that identifies all of the light fittings as symbols plotted on to the drawing. Fixtures and fittings are often shown in a dotted line or in a grey or fine line so that the fitting can be lined up correctly with elements on plan. Ceiling features and rafts will also be indicated.

Principles of lighting

Retail interiors are lit in a very specific way so that the product is illuminated to the best advantage and the journey around the store is highlighted with different layers of brightness and focus. The lighting scheme is generally built up in layers. First is accent lighting, which highlights the product and is the brightest element in the store. Second is task lighting, which is present in the service areas such as the cash desks, fitting rooms or consultation spaces. Third is ambient lighting, which guides the customer around the walkways and does not impact on the lighting of the product or services.

Accent lighting

The shop window plays with the contrast of daylight and artificial light. As the time or season changes, daylight reduces and gives way to the artificial illumination. As the customer approaches the store, the window display is strongly lit to focus the eye and draw the customer in. Once inside the store, the accent lighting is focused on the product using a variety of fittings and techniques. Downlighters in the ceiling wash walls and mid-floor fixtures, and lighting glows internally from LEDs in cabinets, sometimes creating lightboxes behind signage.

Task and feature lighting

The task lighting illuminates cash desks, fitting rooms, seated areas and consultation spaces. The lighting level is dropped slightly so that it does not interfere with the accent lighting, but is bright enough for the customer and staff to see what they are doing. The task lighting may be in the form of a feature light – a pendant or chandelier to highlight the activity below.

Ambient lighting

The ambient lighting's task is to highlight walkways and give a general glow to the space that does not encroach on the accent or task lighting. The lighting over walkways may be recessed into the ceiling or a row of equally spaced pendants. Often the ambient lighting is incorporated into a ceiling feature, such as a lighting trough, for instance.

Light fittings

CDM (CERAMIC DICHARGE METAL HALIDE): This light fitting is incredibly bright and is used in window displays and to wash walls filled with products.

LED (LIGHT EMITTING DIODE): This type of lighting is now used extensively in a wide range of fittings, has a very low heat emission and is energy efficient. The fitting is made up of a series of small bulbs that are very long lasting and can come in a variety of colour temperatures.

LOW-VOLTAGE DOWNLIGHTERS: Low-voltage fittings are used in recessed downlighters. They are used either independently or as secondary

Figure 4.20 **THE WHITE COMPANY Brent Cross, UK DESIGNER, CAULDER MOORE, 2006** This design incorporates a recessed ceiling trough with feature lighting. Branding and Identity. © Caulder Moore

Figure 4.21 **BOLON, Shanghai, CHINA, 2016, Designer Pfarre Lighting Design** This striking showroom is a success in concealed lighting. The main display wall appears to glow with LED lights, concealed in the display fixture to highlight the product. The useof simple materials such as the mirrored ceiling creates drama and enhances the product. © Shuhe Architectural Photography, Beijing via Pfarre Lighting Design

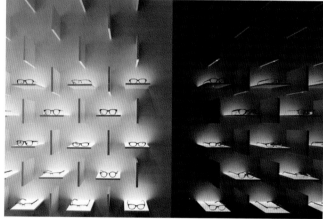

lighting for products and can also be used to wash the interior with ambient light. These fittings should be set at about 750mm apart to give an even glow.

FLUORESCENT: These fittings are very versatile and come in a range of lengths between 300mm and 1500mm long. They can also be circular and come small enough to fit inside cabinets. They can be positioned behind ceiling rafts or wall pelmets, overlapping each other for an even glow of ambient light, or using in back-of-house areas as they are inexpensive and efficient. They have an average lifespan of 12,000–20,000 hours.

TRACK LIGHTING: This is often used when there is little or no ceiling void available to recess a light fitting. They are not the most attractive form of lighting, but are efficient and flexible in certain circumstances.

Figure 4.22 MALL OF SCANDINAVIA Stockholm, SWEDEN DESIGNER, WINGÅRDHS, 2015 This feature lighting installation creates a dramatic atmosphere to this central social space. It allows the lighting to change, allowing welcome daylight throughout day whilst providing a stunning lighting display during what can be long periods of darkness.

It is a good example of the use of LED fittings, which have a long life with little maintenance. © Andre Pihl via Wingardhs

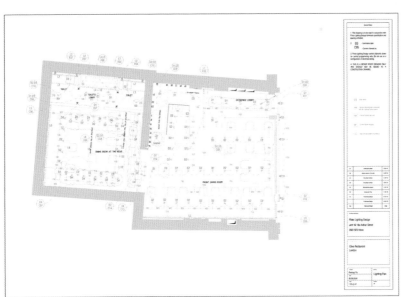

Figure 4.23 A TYPICAL CEILING PLAN INDICATING SERVICES, Olivio Restaurant, Pinto Lighting Design, 2016. This drawing shows a typical reflected ceiling plan for retail. The drawing contains information about light fittings and how they are positioned in relation to the fixtures and fittings. © Pinto Lighting Design

The atmosphere of the interior space can be affected by factors that may seem beyond our control, but they are an essential design consideration within the whole interior scheme. As with all interior projects, designing a space for retail focuses on the customer or user and their comfort within the space.

Interior Comfort is controlled by a number of factors; the temperature in the store, as well as the sounds in the store, become part of the ambience and therefore the overall experience. Decisions are clearly made when selecting materials regarding their acoustic qualities and how that will impact on the feel of the space. Climate control is a necessary part of the services required in retail space and sees the merger of skills between the retail designer and a mechanical engineer in resolving these issues.

Air quality

The temperature of an interior space can affect the overall shopping experience and also, of course, the working environment for staff. Retail designers work closely with mechanical engineers specializing in air-conditioning to meet the required heating and cooling criteria. Once the interior has been proposed, the drawings are passed to the mechanical engineer who then designs the climate control scheme.

The air-conditioning system will consist of ceiling- or wall-mounted units evenly spaced throughout the store and a warm air curtain over the door to relieve the cold draughts coming in from the entrance, which might be permanently open. Each air-conditioning unit is connected to a condenser (most commonly positioned outside), and provides conditioned air or water to the units within the space. Generally the servicing ducts are concealed in the ceiling void where periodic access will be required. Extraction kitchen areas in the case of a café or restaurant will be provided together with ventilation for toilet facilities.

Acoustics

Retail spaces, in most cases, do not have to deal with eliminating high levels of noise from within the space or from the outside leaking in, and can use the simplest forms of acoustic control to enhance the environment. The shopfront acts as a barrier from the exterior to the interior against street noise. The construction of the interior shell will create an acoustic barrier between retail units; in some instances it may be necessary to use an acoustic grade material between the skin of the wall and stud partition.

Figure 4.24 **WHITE COMPANY STORE** Brent Cross, UK **DESIGNER, CAULDER MOORE, 2006** Using a tiled floor and gloss finishes on the walls in this store enhances the sounds of the space and will create echoes of footsteps and conversations, enhancing the acoustic qualities of the space. Acoustic attenuation is balanced by the absorbent qualities of the products on display. © Caulder Moore

The main consideration of acoustics in a retail scheme is that of ambience in terms of the balance of a lively or quiet environment. This might also be augmented by background sounds or music, which will require a design which delivers sound in terms of the balance of hard and soft materials. The main elements for consideration are the walls, floors and ceilings of the space but also the merchandise which may have acoustic qualities of its own.

The use of soundscapes rather than just music is becoming an important part of the retail experience and is increasingly using a range of techniques from areas of crossover such as the theatre and exhibition design.

PETER ZUMTHOR

'Listen! Interiors are like large instruments, collecting sound, amplifying it, transmitting it elsewhere.'

Material audit

Visit a retail site that you are interested in and make notes and photographs of the principal materials in the space, using some of the methods that you have used previously.

Try and identify what the principal materials are, being as precise as possible. Look also at the finish and application of the materials.

Make a simple matrix diagram using images and words describing what you have found.

What impression does this create relative to the brand?

What are the senses are the materials creating?

As an additional exercise you should now examine a brand whose store you have never visited or perhaps doesn't exist, for example an online-only brand.

Using an A3 or A2 sheet begin by collecting images or perhaps real samples of materials that you think are inspired by or communicate the brand you are considering. Also use text to explain why they are appropriate, how they define the brand and their emotional attributes.

Arrange the sheet into a poetic and creative representation of your ideas.

Lighting scheme

From your visit in the previous exercise, draw a simple plan of the space Don't worry too much about the accuracy but try and note all of the key features and fittings. Also make a note of the type of light fittings used; take photos if possible.

Back in the studio draw a scale plan of the layout at 1:50. From your observations try and identify which light fittings are used in the scheme and try to find images of them.

Next, mark the fittings on the plan where you think they are (or should be) to create the scheme you have studied. Use the correct symbols and provide a key, trying to be accurate in your placing of the fittings. If you are able visit the site again and check the accuracy of your observations then you should do so.

Figure 4.25 Jurlique, Adelaide Designer: Landini Associates Using the history of the business as the inspiration the design brings authenticity and tactility into the retail experience using the concept of 'an elegant allotment shed'. Back illuminated panels mimic daylight streaming through frosted glass, whilst a video wall at the back recreates the view into real farm greenhouses. Living plants in trays sit alongside the product, with galvanized watering cans and wooden crates used as props. Point-of-sale is carved onto smooth, chunky wooden blocks.
© Landini Associates

The success of any retail interior does not depend solely on its brand, product or building. The interior layout plays an important role in creating a seamless experience for all visitors. The organization of the space, from the entrance to the way people navigate and use the area beyond, is governed by the layout. This should not encroach on the users; it should not become a conscious part of the overall shopping experience but rather should enhance the quality of the space and the time spent within it.

THIS CHAPTER explores the principles of organizing retail space and gives an insight into the techniques used to create an effective and engaging layout. Taking the idea of the customer journey as the starting point this will be developed for use as a map for strategies that are adopted within the retail environment.

Once the brand has been established and the market and demographic for its products are fully understood, an analysis of the retailer's current building stock or an investigation into finding a suitable site begins. There may be brand guidelines for the interior which will demonstrate a typical size of store for the implementation of the scheme. Although these guidelines set out the rules of layout, they are intended to be adjusted on a site-by-site basis to suit the building (considering its location as well as the interior structure) but the principles within the guide will remain.

The retail designer must also work within the guidelines of local codes and regulations to make sure that the space is accessible to pushchair and wheelchair users and people with other disabilities. Ideally, these necessary considerations appear seamless and incorporated into the overall scheme as part of the design rather than as an addition.

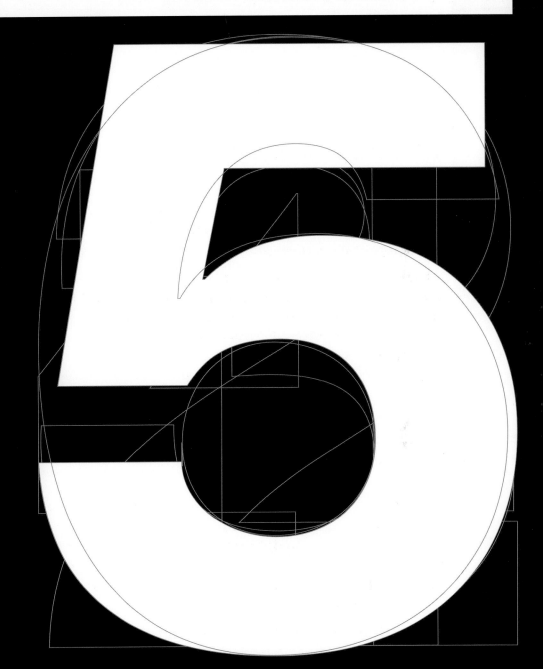

At the earliest stages it is important to define what the particular journey is that you are trying to create and how you want people to move through and engage with the space. This will define how the space is created. In this chapter we will look at how spaces are formed, their uses and activities to create an engaging retail experience.

As part of the initial investigations into the space, and particularly the initial explorations of circulation and movement it is worth considering some of the basic principles of organization of the space.

This will be dependent on a range of criteria but will probably start with an audit of the host space. This may be a new building, a shell such as a unit in a mall or an existing building requiring renovation and repurposing. Each of these may require a different response which should be investigated at the earliest opportunity, ideally before the space is legally secured. In some cases this may involve a retailer who has an extensive existing portfolio of store spaces in which case an audit of these spaces should be carried out prior to or in conjunction with the design process.

It is relatively straightforward to assess criteria such as footprint, location and proximity to other retailers, but intangibles such as style of the building, surroundings and elements such as period features are more difficulty to assess and align more closely with the identity and personality of the brand.

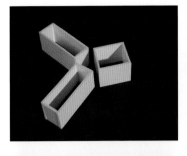
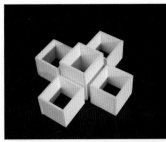
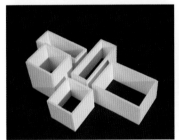
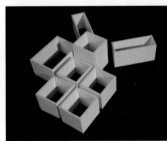

Figure 5.1
Spatial Strategies At the earliest stages of the design it is worth looking at the basic spatial and movement strategies that you wish to adopt, this will provide you with a template for your design. These images have been produced by Ian Higgins from his book *Spatial Strategies* to illustrate examples of how space might be organized. © Ian Higgins

Figure 5.2 Sonos Flagship Store, NY This experience store, which consists of a series of demonstration pavilions adopts a linear spatial strategy which allows customers to easily navigate from one space to the other. Note how the designers have used this configuration to reinforce the brand. © Echochamber

Figures 5.3, 5.4 and 5.5 **LAFAYETTE
MAISON Paris, France Designer, SAGUEZ &
PARTNERS, 2004** Lafayette Maison houses
the home store department within one of
the largest department stores in the world,
Lafayette. The store is laid out so that the
products on each floor correspond with a room
in a house. The basement is the kitchen, selling
cookware and utensils; the ground floor is the
entrance hall where visitors are welcomed in
the large foyer; the first floor is the dining room
containing dining furniture; the second floor is
the living room, stocking essential lounge items;
and the third floor houses the bedroom and
bathroom ranges.

Signage played an important role in the
overall design. The designers needed to ensure
that the layout was easy to navigate, enabling
the customer to wander around and discover
other areas of the store without getting lost.

The atrium is the central focus, with
horizontal movement around the periphery
and open views through all windows. The tills
and service desks always remain in the same
position and furniture displays are arranged so
as not to interrupt views through the building.
© Luc Boegly/Saguez and Partners

We have moved rapidly from the store as a space to sell things to more of a space that sells experiences, reinforcing the narrative and stories of the particular brand. We need to understand this and use it to design the customer journey through the store.

As we have seen in Chapter 1, there is no one single customer journey but a variety of ways of creating an engaging experience whereby the customer feels part of the experience and in some cases may be creating the actual experience. This will create a number of variations depending on the requirements of the customer and what is being sold which might be type of product, experience or service.

From this we can simplify the areas within the retail interior as the key elements of any design together with some of the variations that will occur with various retail formats.

Taking the terms adopted from Chapter 1 these have been broken down into the following common areas within the store:

> Recognition: The external identity

> Welcome: The approach and entrance

> Immersion and Exploration: The store experience, circulation, pace and display, engagement and interaction spaces

Retail spaces

In the modern interconnected omni channel retail environment the design of the layout must create a meaningful and authentic narrative for the visitor, this will vary from brand to brand and perhaps even within different store formats. The ability to engage the customer at every stage of the journey is of key importance in order to bring people through the store.

Recognition

Our approach to the store and particularly its relationship with the surrounding buildings and environment are particularly important. We may recognise the identity from a distance but as we approach the building we will be conscious of the complimentary identities that surround it.

Entrance and welcome

The design of the entrance to a store is very important. It needs to entice the customer in and provide a glimpse of the products beyond the threshold. The design of the shopfront is discussed in more detail in Chapter 6. In general though, it will be either a new element – fitted as part of the overall scheme – or an existing element preserved in its original form or updated to meet building and planning regulations. Window displays are regularly updated to show the latest products in the store although increasingly

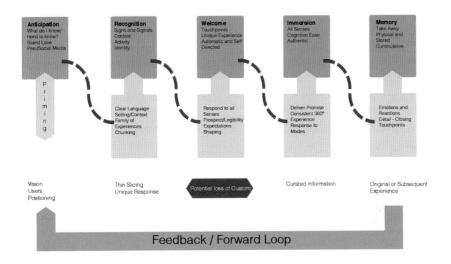

| **Anticipation**
What do I know/
need to know?
Brand Love
Peer/Social Media | **Recognition**
Signs and Signals
Context
Activity
Identity | **Welcome**
Touchpoints
Unique Experience
Automatic and Self
Directed | **Immersion**
All Senses
Cognitive Ease
Authentic | **Memory**
Take Away
Physical and
Stored
Cummulative |

Priming

| | Clear Language
Setting/Context
Family of
Experiences
Chunking | Respond to all
Senses
Prospect/Legibility
Expectations
Shaping | Deliver Promise
Consistent 360°
Experience
Response to
Modes | Emotions and
Reactions
Detail - Closing
Touchpoints |

| Vision
Users
Positioning | Thin Slicing
Unique Response | Potential loss of Custom | Curated Information | Original or Subsequent
Experience |

Feedback / Forward Loop

Figure 5.6 CUSTOMER JOURNEY In the diagram in Figure 5.6 the key stages of the customer journey are aligned with the key areas within the space; these are studied in detail over the following pages.

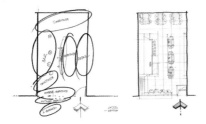

Figures 5.7 and 5.8 GOOD AND PROPER, Designer 2020, 2016 These diagrams for a new tea room concept illustrate how the space is organized, starting with simple sketches outlining the activities and how they will be organized through to the plan and visual of how the concept might be realized. © Guy Archard via 20-20

the layering of the interior will allow customers to see past the window displays to the store beyond, allowing transparency and interaction. However there is a growing trend for the exterior to be a foil or mask for the interior, perhaps communicating a different message or providing a feeling of mystery and secrecy known only to those that the brand is focussed towards.

Once beyond the threshold, the welcome space is the starting point of the interior journey. It is an area of the store that is often left open and spacious, giving the customer time to pause and take in the store environment and to make way for people entering and exiting the store comfortably. In larger stores this may be a place to meet friends before or after shopping, sometimes with seating areas outside of the main flow of traffic.

The entrance is a key main area for featuring both the brand story and new season trends or product launches. This could be in the form of a feature display, or a promotional event

Figures 5.9 and 5.10 **COMME DES GARCON POCKET STORE, NY** Taking over an existing retail unit, here the expression of the brand is muted externally, suggested by the polka dot motif which is expressed more obviously in the interior. The shopfront maintains its original format and is designed to be both intriguing and recognizable to those that are familiar with the brand. © Patrick Murdock

including food tasting, or increasingly, this may be aligned to alliances that the brand has with art or sporting events.

The design of the entrance also has to consider access for all users. The entrance must be wide enough for wheelchair and pushchair users and easy for them to manoeuvre. In an existing site, the entrance may be stepped and a ramp may need to encroach into the interior; this needs to be planned as part of the overall scheme.

It has been identified by Paco Underhill that customers need time to acclimatize themselves once they enter a store, this can be used by retailers to provide a transition or decompression zone where brands can prepare customers for the experience.

Figure 5.11 APPLE STORE, LONDON, Architects Foster + Partners, 2016 The spacious welcome area allows visitors to rest and relax, engaging with the brand in their own way and pace. The area is both a social space and a retail space, allowing interaction with products and a welcome rest from the busy street outside. © Leon Neal/Getty Images

> **PACO UNDERHILL: AUTHOR OF *WHY WE BUY: THE SCIENCE OF SHOPPING***
>
> 'What can we do with the transition zone? You can greet customers – not necessarily steer them anywhere but say hello, remind them where they are, start the seduction.'

Immersion and exploration

The ability of the customer to navigate and move freely through the space, referred to as legibility, is of paramount importance; they need to feel in control and able to explore and engage at their own pace.

Circulation

One of the first tasks in the design process is to work out the circulation around the space, taking into consideration the design guidelines and principles of the scheme alongside the structural nature of the interior. Circulation diagrams are produced as ways of thinking and describing different schemes to the client. The diagrams are produced by looking at the plans and sections of the interior and drawing arrows and routes over the technical drawings. The circulation plan is often drawn in unison with an adjacency plan (often on the same drawing), which shows how the areas of the space will be divided into product, places to sell, space to browse and ancillary areas. These drawings form the starting point for planning the interior layout.

The circulation performs two main tasks in the retail scheme. The first is to allow for the flow of people in the form of walkways. These must be wide enough for at least two people to pass each other comfortably, whether walking or in a wheelchair, or pushing a pram. The second, and perhaps most important task, is to reinforce the journey connecting the key spaces, allowing for ample space to browse without bumping into other people or displays.

The principles of circulation are quite simple and are governed by the ways in which people move around the space. There are many ways that this can happen but each is based around a handful of solutions, some of which are illustrated in Figure 5.12.

Circulation can work horizontally, allowing the customer access through the shopfront, with products displayed on either side of the walkway and with an exit at the back; or vertically, with merchandise displayed over more than one floor. This scheme is more complicated in the sense that stairs, lifts and escalators need to be negotiated, and methods for enticing people on to the upper floors must be considered.

Vertical circulation

This is key to the success of any multi-level retail unit and may range from transporting people through several levels in a shopping centre or transport interchange through to linking two levels in a single retail unit. It should be considered as more than just a method of moving people between two levels but an opportunity to enhance the

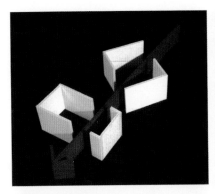

A pass-through-space circulation

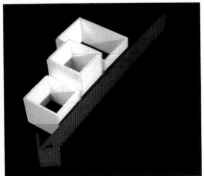

A pass-by-space circulation

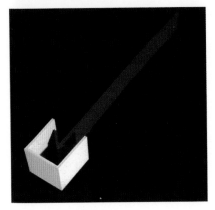

A terminate-in-a-space circulation

Figure 5.12 CIRCULATION DIAGRAMS, Ian Higgins There are several ways of moving through a space and some of the key methods are illustrated here. Each method produces a variety of options for engaging the customer.

These images have been produced by Ian Higgins from his book *Spatial Strategies* to illustrate examples of how space might be organized. © Ian Higgins

experience and perhaps provided a rest from the retail 'noise'.

There are several factors that can be used to enhance and encourage visitors to move vertically through the store, these include:

- Product category mix
- Use of food and beverage as an attractor, particularly in mall environments.
- Leisure or entertainment offers

One of the important aspects is visibility in order that customers can make clear decisions about how they can move through the store to facilitate their journey. In some cases the vertical circulation, particularly escalators, are used as a feature within the space.

Pace

Pace is an interesting aspect of circulation design that analyzes how people use the space as well as move

Figure 5.13 **BARNEYS New York** In this world-famous department store the spiral staircase forms both a sculptural and also visible element which clearly indicates a vertical route through the store. Legibility is particularly important in large stores to allow customers to create their own journey through the space.
© Echochamber

Figure 5.14 **MALL OF SCANDINAVIA Stockholm, SWEDEN Designer, WINGÅRDHS, 2015** Elements such as escalators offer an opportunity to create visual drama within the space, particularly when enhanced through the design of the lighting. © Johan Tägtström via Wingardhs

around it. Pace is very much influenced by the nature of the user, their intentions and modes of shopping, which is one reason why it is important to understand the market targeted by the brand and the area in which the store will be located.

Coffee shops are a good example for describing how pace plays a part in the overall plan of the interior as it often considers many paces within the scheme and is marketed at different types of user groups. The fast-paced user will want to buy a take-away coffee and exit the shop immediately. This is why most large chain coffee shops have a service counter that works very much like a production line. The medium-paced user will go through this service process, then they will sit in the shop to drink and eat their purchase. They might stay for a maximum time of twenty minutes although as laptop use increases so does the time people spend in the space. This seating area is usually located at the front of the shop, in the form of high stools at the windows or on chairs around small tables.

The slow-paced user purchases food and drink and sits for a longer period, often on comfortable chairs and sofas with access to newspapers. These users may stay for an hour or so to meet friends or have their lunch break at a comfortable setting away from the frenetic service area. One of the big attractions for customers here is free wifi, particularly in the main seating areas.

In smaller retail stores, pace may not be an issue, but larger stores such as department stores consider the nature of the users and provide a number of entrances and exits for a quick purchase as well as a more meandering experience.

In some instances this may be simply the distribution of product categories within the space but as we move towards the store as experience every space within the store becomes important and has to play its part in the complete experience

Understanding the product and the necessary quantities needed on display and in immediate storage is paramount to successful merchandising. Retailers' stock tends to change on a regular basis, so flexibility is the key to a functional display fixture. The positioning of merchandise within the interior is very important. Retailers understand their key products and what draws their customers in. The retail designer must use this wealth of knowledge and experience to arrange the products throughout the store so that the customer is enticed from one area to another on a particular journey.

In the design manual, the retailer's merchandising principles are set out as part of the branding and marketing agenda. The retailer may have very specific requirements depending on the merchandise and the range of other related products. Most large retailers have an in-house merchandising team who spend their time working with the products in a generic space (usually in the retailer's main branch office) and deriving solutions to displaying the items effectively. Many products work in collections. Fashion and clothing is

a good example of this, where the clothes and related accessories need to be displayed together.

Product display

Taking up a large part of the retail designer's remit is the design of fixture displays.

In many retail environments this will be a key focus but will take a variety of forms in order to engage, inform and allow the customer to interact. Some displays will be both informational and inspirational which is reflected in the product being centre stage. In other cases product may be used to show the full range that is that is available in terms of size, colour and style.

In any event the fixturing must work to display the product in the appropriate manner and should always play a supporting role. Where possible they should offer a degree of flexibility to allow for future proofing in terms of future product and elements such as technology.

Some fixtures can be bought in a kit form and either used directly in this state, or adjusted with finishes to suit the interior design; other fixtures are custom made. Custom-made pieces work particularly well if the scheme is to be rolled out; the cost of making the fixtures becomes cheaper with larger production quantities. For one-off stores, an off-the-shelf system may be a better solution. These elements, although not at the forefront of the consumer's

Figure 5.15 **FONDACO DEI TEDESCHI, Venice, OMA, 2016** This area tells a clear product story with inspirational display supported by a range of product displays which act as a signpost for the product categories. © Stephen Anderson

Figure 5.16 **TIMBERLAND STORE, London, UK, Designer Dalziel & Pow, 2016** There is an increasing move towards allowing visitors to customize the products that they buy either in-store or for later delivery. In this store there is a section where customers can add customized elements to their purchases such as a range of coloured laces and other additional accessories. © Dalziel & Pow

experience, are the vehicles that drive the interior scheme and make the space function and sell products. Products can be displayed in a variety of interesting ways, but can be broken down into two different types: wall display and mid-floor fixtures.

Using the interior walls is one of the main ways to display products. Go into most retail spaces and the walls will be lined from floor to ceiling with goods. The only instance where this may not be seen is in the premium retail sector as smaller amounts of product are displayed to give a feeling of exclusivity. The principle of the design of the wall fixture is simple. They tend to be (and should have the ability to be) constructed from panels so that they can hold an array of hooks and hangers that can be adjusted to suit any situation. The retail designer will make the wall fixtures unique to the scheme through its material finish. The wall allows for a high level of stock over a large surface, which frees up the central spaces for circulation and feature displays. Between the standard bays are opportunities to make feature statements through specialist displays and graphics.

The mid-floor fixtures consist of a selection of different elements that create interest and stagger the customer's view so that glimpses of the stock behind can be seen. The fixtures could be in the form of tables, cabinets or free-standing gondolas, or could be wrapped around a column, for instance.

: **WILLIAM GREEN**

'Display areas are at the heart of a retail store. Display is the mechanism that presents the merchandise to the shopper in its most favourable light and that permits the shopper to evaluate and select products for purchase.'

Engagement

In addition to the main merchandise displays stores are increasingly incorporating all of the space available to tell their particular brand stories. This is enlivening the whole of the retail environment and allows for a continuity of the experience. In some instances these spaces are sited within the retail space; in other situations good use is made of space that has traditionally not been seen to be naturally productive space.

Limbo spaces

With continually rising rents for space it is important that the total space is used to communicate and enhance the experience.

This has spurred a shift in the dynamics of the store, transforming formerly unused spaces such as staircases, lobbies and even landing areas to contribute and enhance the overall experience. They can be used to create additional narratives such as legacy or vintage displays much like you might view at an exhibition.

Figure 5.17 SUPERDRY London, UK Designer, Nulty In this environment lighting is used to create drama and interest. The overall ambient level is low with the product clearly highlighted; fixtures are also used to create sculptural elements within the space. This approach helps customers navigate the space. © Nulty

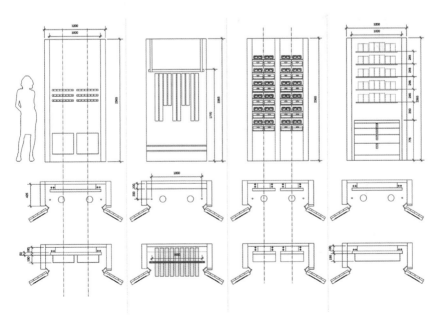

Figure 5.18 MULBERRY Various locations Designer, FOUR IV, 2008 This is a sheet of technical drawings showing the variations of wall 'wardrobe' displays for Mulberry stores. © Four IV

Figure 5.19
FRITZ HANSEN REPUBLIC SHOWROOM, London, UK
Designer, BDP
2011 The staircase can be more than a means of moving between levels. The design of this staircase includes an extended landing space which can be used for display and as a position to rest and appreciate internal and external views. © BDP

Figure 5.20
TFONDACO DEI TEDESCHI, Venice, OMA, 2016 Utilizing an area which forms part of the escalator lobby allows for the display of a range of products and which also includes media elements.
© Stephen Anderson

Engagement spaces

In order to develop and nurture the customer's relationship with the brand, one of the key roles of the retail environment is that of engagement and interaction with the brand. These range from passive in terms of 'on call when required' through to active engagement in a range of experiences. One of the earliest and most striking examples of these is REI Sports in Seattle, which has a climbing wall in its flagship store. Other retailers have used these to good effect to create spaces where customers can test and trial the products to activity spaces where a community spirit can be shared.

Figure 5.21 REI Flagship, Seattle This rock climbing wall forms a truly interactive component and also creates a recognizable form both internally and externally. Customers can use the wall to try out equipment before they purchase. © Wolfgang Kaehler/LightRocket via Getty Images

Figure 5.22 LULU LEMON, London, Designer DALZIEL & POW, 2017 This Lululemon store in central London offers events such as yoga classes, creating a sense of belonging and community amongst its customers. The ethos was to create a community hub where people could learn and discuss the physical aspects of healthy living and mindfulness.

Sports brands such as Nike and Rapha offer group running and cycling training in the evening. © Dalziel & Pow

Transformation spaces

These are flexible spaces that can literally be easily changed and transfigured to create a range of different formats. Many of these encourage the user to arrange objects much like they would in their home. For example the IKEA Apartment in Warsaw, Poland hosts dinner parties and other social events.

Customer service spaces – payment and customer service

In many instances the point of sale marks the end of the journey around the store and is the point at which a customer will pay for goods. In larger stores, there will be access to till points in several locations, often relating to a department; one in menswear and one in womenswear, for example. In supermarkets, the till points are usually located in front of the exit doors. In smaller stores, the till point or cash desk can be located in a number of places: at the back of the store, with a feature wall behind it so that it can be seen from the shopfront; halfway into the store along a side wall, dividing the product display; or at the front of the store, close to the entrance and marking the end of the shopping experience. Also, positioning the till point by the entrance of a small store where there may only be one or two members of staff working is advantageous. The entrance/exit can be watched by the staff from the till to deter shoplifters.

Whilst the payment point is still an important feature within the store through technology such as Apple Pay and contactless systems this activity can now be performed throughout the store. In addition, retail staff are now required to fulfil a number of roles including that of a brand ambassador as retailers have realized that these staff are an important touchpoint to the brand. Many retail environments such as Apple stores promote engagement through a simple legible layout and the ability for customers to engage with both product and staff. This seamless interaction is further enhanced by arranging seminars and workshops together with mobile payment through an iPhone app, which is beginning to be adopted by many brands such as Adidas.

However, with the advent of customer facilities such as 'click and collect' together with an increase in the theatrical and presentational aspects of retail it is important that fixtures are created to facilitate this.

As well as being a place to pay for goods, the point of sale also holds a merchandising opportunity with 'impulse' buys such as chocolate, stamps or small accessory items.

More recently in some retail instances, the point of sale may be a self-service coin/card machine. These devices are increasingly being used in supermarkets, petrol stations and train stations to provide a quicker service at peak times.

Seamless integration of technology

As we move towards an omni channel experience in retail stores seamlessly linking together a variety of interactive channels, technology is no longer a bolt-on or afterthought but should be an integral part of the interior experience.

**Figure 5.23
CASH DESK
POSITION** These drawings depict the various positions of the cash desk and how they sit alongside the merchandise and work with the circulation. The design of the cash desk coincides with the overall design scheme. It is often well lit and easy to see from all around the store. © Dalziel & Pow

Figure 5.24 JIGSAW ST JAMES EMPORIUM, London, Designer Dalziel & Pow, 2014 This simple customer point enhances the slightly industrial aesthetic of the building and has a simple sculptural form. Any technology is hidden within the element which allows it to function in a number of ways and create a presence within the space. © Dalziel & Pow

There are currently a range of emerging technologies which include beacon tracking technology, elements such as flooring which can track and encourage movement patterns, sensory responses to visitor movement such as sound, vision and smell, together with a range of flexible environmental responses to respond to user desires. Through these processes retailers increasingly collect an ever-increasing amount of data about their customers which they will analyze to help provide a more individual and tailored response to customers, which may range from purchasing decisions to more focussed areas such as fitness in sports retail.

In addition to the main retail display area there will also be dedicated space for customer support; these spaces may consist of fitting rooms and staff/customer consultation areas. The design of these spaces is just as important as that of the main display space. Because they are used by the public they are carefully considered in order that they work alongside the branded interior in terms of finish and graphics, and so that they convey a positive image of the customer service.

Public toilets are often provided in larger retail stores and again these are an important part of the customer experience. This is particularly true in large department stores and retail malls where they help extend customer visits.

Fitting rooms

In fashion stores, fitting rooms are essential for customers to 'try before they buy'. These have been an area of focus and most retailers now favour separate spacious cubicles for changing with mirrors on all sides, a fixed seat, hooks for your own clothes and bags, sometimes with a lockable door for added discretion.

In larger stores, this space contains seating and sometimes even entertainment for those who have to wait. In smaller stores that do not have the space to do this, the most basic entrance will have a rail for unwanted items and sometimes a

sales assistant to help and log the clothes that are being tried on (fitting rooms are one of the main places where shoplifting occurs).

Another aspect of fitting room design that is important is lighting. The positioning of the light fitting in relation to the mirror and the colour of the light shining on to bare skin can be unflattering and would not aid a sale. As technology has progressed, fitting room lighting has taken a different approach, with many cubicles containing a switch so that the customer can adjust the lighting levels and colour to suit.

Every clothing store must have a fitting room equipped for customers with disabilities. The room must be large enough to take a wheelchair; it must have grab rails and a strategically placed mirror as well as a seat. In very small stores, it is acceptable to have just one changing cubicle, but it must comply with disability rights and relevant local codes.

SAGUEZ & PARTNERS

'. . . you need to catch your breath, need a meeting point, somewhere to sit down, to take a break. . . and clean toilets where you can redo your makeup, a left-luggage facility to leave your packages while you carry on shopping, refreshment areas, a car park, a deliveries area . . .'

Customer toilets

In department stores and supermarkets, the provision of customer toilet facilities is essential, especially if the store contains eating or refreshment facilities. Some treat these areas like back of house with basic fittings and finishes, whilst others choose to continue the branding into the toilets. The design and choice of cubicle partitions and sanitary ware, as well as floor and wall finishes, depend on their durability and easiness to clean as they are very well used and are sometimes subject to vandalism. If customer toilets are offered, then facilities for disabled customers must also be provided.

Service areas

This area is the part of the store that the customer never sees. It is almost always positioned at the back of the store so that it is located off the service area behind the shop unit for easy access for deliveries and removing packaging and other waste from site. There is often a door that leads directly to the service area from the back of the store so that deliveries aren't taken through the main shop. This door can also act as a secondary fire escape from the building and it is important to make sure that the hallway from the store to the rear exit is wide and without obstacles.

Within the service area there will be, at the least, a staff room containing a basic kitchen with microwave, kettle and table and chairs, staff toilets (this could be one disabled cubicle for small stores, or a separate male and female facility), perhaps a small manager's

Figure 5.25
SELFRIDGES BODY STUDIO FITTING ROOMS London, UK Designer: Neri & Hu, Lighting by Nulty, 2016 The design of these fitting rooms provides a sensual and relaxing experience reflecting the ambience of this particular area with the store and continues the shopping experience.
© Nulty

Figure 5.26 **PACIFIC PLACE Hong Kong, Designer HEATHERWICK STUDIO, 2011** As part of an upgrade and extension of this mall these public washrooms provide a feeling of both luxury and warmth through the use of indirect lighting and timber panels.
© Heatherwick Studio

office and a stockroom. The size of the stockroom will depend on the retail business and using a standard storage system, some of which come with mezzanine constructions to take full advantage of the height of the space. The finish to this area tends to be basic but durable, using cost-effective materials throughout.

Spatial audit

You should begin this exercise by choosing a particular category or type of store, for example fashion, technology or perhaps a larger format such as DIY and homewares. Visit a range before you make your decision.

Once you have decided on your store type visit a typical example of this and use the observational methods used in the previous chapters. You should be paying particular attention to the following aspects of the store.

Journey   Circulation   Key Spaces

Imagine yourself as both a potential customer but also someone who is simply browsing.

Following your visit create a diagram or map of what you discovered from your visit, you may use through the following process:

> Draw a simple block plan of the main space(s) in proportion.

> Identify the spatial systems and circulation paths that were adopted.

> Next begin to fill in the detail such as the key events and spaces, trying to identify these from the examples in the text.

> Add as much detail as you can to produce a complete picture, using a combination of words, images and sketches.

As an extension to this exercise you should now think of an imaginary brand that you would like to design for, perhaps within the category chosen in the first part of this exercise or applied to a project that you are working on.

Think about the experience that you would like to create for this brand and how you might apply this to a physical layout.

Draw a repeat the previous exercise but now apply this to the brand that you have created and bring your ideas to life.

Figure 5.27 Missguided, Bluewater, Kent, UK Designer: Dalziel & Pow, 2017 Located in the Bluewater shopping mall this store bursts out of its confines to attract attention and bring customers seamlessly in to explore the interior. The brand is fearless, fun and self expressive which is reflected in the design environment, use of elements such as large mirrors seek to blur the boundary between store and mall.
© Dalziel & Pow

The area where retail really comes to life is in the detail, and no more so than the oft-used phrase 'retail is detail'. This should encompass every area of the experience from the initial arrival through to the customers' memories when leaving the store. Every component within this experience needs to align with the expectations and values of the particular brand for that environment.

THIS CHAPTER **examines the key elements that the designer needs to consider: the architecture of each building or site; the role of the shopfront and how its configuration and style impacts on the interior scheme; the interior structure and the elements of the design scheme that work within it to form the interior envelope, together with the fixtures, fittings and components.**

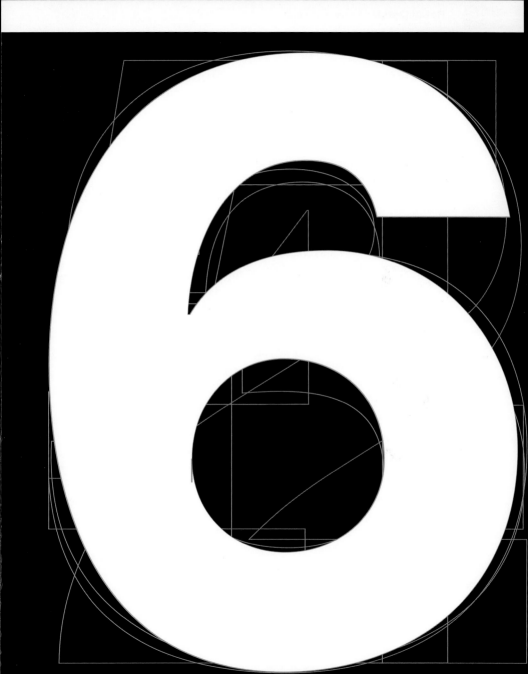

Before we look at the elements of the retail space in detail it is worth looking at the principal elements and how they combine and contribute to the whole experience.

Recognition   Retail Façade – The Retail Façade and Shopfront

Welcome   Interior Envelope – Walls, Floors and Ceilings

Immersion   Display and Events – Foreground, Mid- and Background

Whilst these all combine to create the total experience in this chapter we will look in detail about how they each contribute to this whole.

Retail façade – the shopfront

This is many visitors' first impression of the store and it is shaped by its immediate context such as the building it sits within and its position within the retail street or mall.

The shopfront's main task is to communicate to potential customers the essence of the interior and to display a glimpse of what can be found within. In most cases, the shopfront is designed to make customers feel comfortable when approaching the store and venturing over the threshold. For others, the shop window can be used as visual promotion, particularly at night and holiday periods.

In some instances, the shopfront and entrance are designed to deter the public from entering, with security on the door, having to ring a bell at the entrance or needing an appointment to enter. This particular method is sometimes used in premium retail where exclusivity and wealth are expected.

There are many considerations that need to be made when designing a shopfront. The shop façade must communicate the essence of the brand. This is done through graphic communication: fascia signage, a projecting sign, window details and lifestyle graphics as part of the window displays; the materials from which a new shopfront is constructed, or how an existing shopfront can be adapted to meet the design requirements; the merchandise in the window and the brand message that is conveyed by the window display; and the position of the entrance door and how this will be managed.

As part of the interior design manual for the retailer, a variety of shopfront configurations may be explored. The approach to shopfront design will vary depending on the site location and the impact of the design of the neighbouring shop façades, as well as planning and listed building requirements. Also, the retailer will have obligations to the landlord; a contract will generally be drawn up between the two regarding

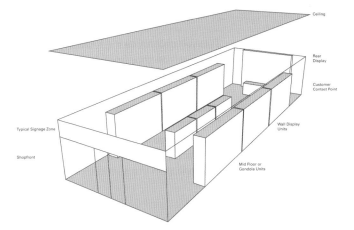

Figure 6.1 Key Interior Elements The diagram in Figure 6.1 is useful in looking at how we experience a retail space and the components that contribute to this. From this the elements have been grouped together to create a response to some the stages of experience discussed previously.

Figure 6.2 LULU LEMON, London, Designers DALZIEL & POW, 2016 In this store all of the key components of the interior are clearly articulated. The space has been stripped back to provide a clear legible space into which elements of lighting, display and customer interaction have been carefully inserted. There is an honesty about the space which is reinforced through carefully designed services which have generally been exposed.
© Dalziel & Pow

each other's responsibility to the unit or building. If the shopfront is to be retained, this contract will state the conditions.

In shopping centres there are considerations as to where the retail brand and the centre brand reinforce each other and typically there are design guides which regulate the design and materials to be used on a particular shopfront.

Although the design of the shopfront varies from site to site, within the rules of the location guidelines, there are

SHONQUIS MONERO

'A pane of glass. . . divides the shop from the pavement. On one side, the climate-controlled interior welcomes those who can buy; on the other, the intemperate street is where those who cannot buy may look without paying – in the timehonoured tradition of window-shopping.'

common principles and techniques that are applied. There are several responses that a designer might adopt at this early stage:

- Maintain the existing shopfront
- Modify the existing shopfront
- Create a new shopfront

This will determine the relationship between the shopfront, the building and the retail interior. It may be governed by a variety of factors, for example the building might be protected by listing, the retailer might want to exist within the language of the site or might want to create something that is radically different from the surroundings.

Figures 6.3, 6.4 and 6.5 **Approaches to the Shopfront** These examples show a variety of approaches to the design of a shopfront within an existing building. They generally respect the existing architectural style whilst increasing visibility. The use of a canopy and planting creates a semi private area which can be used for customer seating. © Stephen Anderson

Existing shopfront

This may be a decision made based on how the brand wishes to communicate itself or a response to local codes and is sometimes a combination of both.

There are a range of responses here which may range from the brands desire to appear part of the community to reasons of planning where there are specific guidelines about what can be designed. If this is the case, then restrictions may also be in place regarding the application of signage and the colour in which the shopfront can be painted. In some instances, a standard font, text size and colour may be specified as well as the type of signage. Signage may have to be painted onto the fascia rather than applied on a fascia box, and a standard projecting sign to match all others in the area or mall may be part of the conditions.

Modification of existing shopfront

This is probably the most common form of design where elements of the existing shopfront or façade are retained but modified to reflect conditions such as improved customer access, visibility or the inclusion of signage or additional elements such as awnings.

It is also common for a new or recreated shopfront to be fitted within an existing opening.

Creation of a new shopfront

The creation of a new shopfront allows the designer to create an element that reflects what the brand is communicating. This provides the designer with a blank canvas open to a variety of responses; the choice might be to create a seamless glazed response which almost feels invisible through to the creation of a unique vision which is very specific to the brand.

Figure 6.6 FULLCIRCLE London, UK, 2008 This shopfront has a large opening directly onto the shopping mall, making the transition from the walkway into the store seamless. © Alex Franklin courtesy of Brinkworth

Internal/external shop front

The designer faces different design opportunities and solutions depending on whether the store is in an internal setting such as a shopping centre, arcade or retail outlet or if it is directly on the street. The design of the internal shopfront in a mall, for example, does not have to consider weather conditions and so can be of a more open design. The entrance into the unit may have a shutter for security without a solid door behind and may be very wide – some are the width of the entire frontage. Also, the internal shopfront, depending on the guidelines of the shopping centre, will probably have an area in front of the unit called a 'pop-out zone', which is usually about 500–1000 mm deep. This means that part of the shopfront design can literally pop out into the mall. This technique is used to create visual differences between shop units and is used when shopping centres want to encourage differentiation in shopfront design.

The external shopfront has to be completely secure and weatherproof and will have solid lockable access, probably with a roller shutter, either just in front of the door or the whole frontage. The shopfront will also have to sit comfortably with its neighbours and possibly the whole row, in order to comply with fascia panel rules and guidelines. This restricts opportunities to play with the design.

Window displays and signage

The shop window begins with a pane of glass that creates a division between the exterior and the interior. In most new shopfronts, the glazing covers as large an area as possible, so much so that the division barely exists. Display design is a profession in its own right, with new concepts reaching windows on a cyclical basis.

The purpose of the display is to create a memorable vision and to portray the brand values in one punchy statement. The display must be consistent with the interior and product range in the materials used, the way the display is lit and the graphic communication. The window suggests the lifestyle that can be achieved from owning the products and entices the customer inside. The size of the window display and the way the merchandise is set out must be coherent to the products displayed. For instance, larger items need a spacious window so that the shopper can stand back to look, whilst smaller items need to be displayed at eye level so that the shopper can walk up close and view them without bending or stretching.

Most window displays are designed around a shallow plinth that raises the merchandise to an appropriate height in relation to the glazing, and allows for mannequins, price statements and additional blocks to be added for smaller products. The retailer's merchandising team usually sources mannequins, but occasionally the retail designer will advise them. It has become increasingly common for retailers to use the window display as a strong statement akin to an art installation.

The design of shopfront signage is often governed by the location of the site and any conditions applied by landlords,

Figure 6.7 SIZE? Bristol, UK Designer, CHECKLAND KINDLEYSIDES, 2009 This unique shopfront has a black-and-white photograph applied to the façade. Inspired by its location in The Horsefair, Bristol, the signage of this shopfront thus takes direct reference from the store's locality.
© Checkland Kindleysides

centre management or planning. There are a variety of options available for each situation. The retail designer will work with a signage manufacturer to come up with suitable solutions. The main signage types are fascia sign, projecting sign and window decals.

The design of the fascia sign may appear varied on the high street, but they commonly fall under one of three types of signage: the traditional painted sign; an illuminated box sign that is constructed most commonly from an aluminium frame with the logo or lettering fret cut out of the face and replaced with frosted acrylic (the box contains fluorescent light fittings that are easily accessible by the panel) and, finally, a logo or letters that have been fret cut out of a sheet of aluminium or steel (possibly spray painted or brushed) that are then projected off the fascia panel and often illuminated from an external source.

The projecting sign, in a similar fashion, can either be a traditional painted sign or an illuminated box sign (constructed in the same way as the fascia sign) suspended from a steel frame bolted into the shopfront.

Window decals are applied to announce promotions or short-life messages as they can easily be replaced. A decal is a graphic made from vinyl that is applied directly to the glass at eye level and is there to stop people from walking through the glass. Most retailers stick to a simple decal that does not detract from the view into the shop and makes the glass look as though it is frosted, whilst others create a graphic statement over the entire window. The vinyl is self-adhesive and can be easily removed.

The principle surfaces which shape the form of the retail space are the key elements which communicate the feel of the space. They provide the structure for materials and display as well as incorporating functions such as lighting, security and services.

Part of the retail designer's job is to survey the site before producing the drawing package for the implementation of the retail scheme. This may be to check dimensions from drawings that may have already been obtained, or it could be to carry out a full survey so that an existing set of drawings can be produced. Depending on the complexities of the site, it may be preferable to employ an architect or surveyor to undertake this task.

As retail sites tend to change hands frequently, there are often anomalies within the building's structure where major work may need to be done to reconfigure the interior to suit the new scheme. With this in mind, the design solutions are often left open to compromise. This is the challenge facing any interior designer working within an existing building.

It is sometimes desirable to retain the architectural details created or maintained by others and working with them is the most environmentally

Figure 6.8 SKANDIUM HOME, London, Designers: Stephen Anderson with PATH, 2017 As visitors enter the store the welcome space allows for rest and refreshment; the area includes exhibition elements as well as themed promotions. From this space all floors are visible and this creates legibility and allows customers to choose the areas they wish to visit. © Path Design

friendly solution. Sometimes this will not work and, understandably, the site will be stripped out.

In retail, the term 'architecture' tends to refer to the fabric of the building: walls, floors and ceilings. These are all elements that become part of the overall scheme, but in many cases remain a neutral backdrop against which to display the main brand elements. The integration of this with the merchandise display and events within the store are key to a successful retail environment.

Retail design often employs a variety of strategies with the interior space, creating a stage for the performance of the brand, or a façade masking the true architecture of the space.

G. BROOKER & S. STONE

'. . . they are re-modelled, reused, rethought and yet a suggestion of the former meaning disturbs and inspires the subsequent design . . .'

Figure 6.9 **LOBLAWS, Toronto, Canada Designer: Landini Associates, 2011** Here the existing building has been stripped back to expose the raw structure of brick and cast concrete. The new elements such as the sculpture and escalator have been inserted as a contrast but also as an announcement of the new environment below.

This is a successful blend of the existing and the new intervention utilizing the industrial scale of the original space. © Loblaws MLG by Landini Associates landiniassociates.com. Photograph by Trevor Mein

Walls

These are the key defining elements of the space and can consist of structural walls which support the building structurally and generally divide units or principle spaces, and partition walls which offer greater flexibility in terms of construction and integration of, say, display elements.

Walls can be used to display vast amounts of products, create feature displays and have colour, texture and pattern applied to them in a variety of finishes. Many retail designers use the wall to carry the design concept through the scheme. Walls can act as dividers between product offers or areas, as a piece of sculpture in its own right, or to add focus to a space.

Figure 6.10 **VERTU STORE London, UK Designer, SHED DESIGN, 2007** This wall feature cleverly holds product, recessed and lit within a black strip. The feature is architecturally interesting and suits the brand concept. The ceiling feature sits above the central space and highlights the car displayed below. The ceiling 'floats' and a recessed lighting feature appears like a shaft of daylight, spilling into life. © Shed

Floors

In many respects flooring can be used as the principal design plane to both encourage visitors into the store and also to move and navigate them through the space once inside. There is an increasing use of the floor as a graphic messaging device but also new technologies allow both monitoring of movement and encouragement of movement through interactive elements within smart flooring systems.

The choice of finishes in this area are large and ever increasing and it is important that the designer adopts the correct selection criteria. They might consider aspects such as durability, sustainability and any regulatory aspects such as slip resistance in a potentially wet environment.

Figure 6.11 SELFRIDGES BODY STUDIO FITTING ROOMS London, UK Designer, Neri & Hu, Lighting by Nulty, 2016 These striking timber ceiling elements create interest through light and texture. They also help to create discrete zones in the retail space. © Nulty

Floors come in a variety of materials and finishes, but the key to a retail floor is durability. The expected lifespan of a floor finish can be anything from five to twenty years depending on the retailer's needs. The quality of the floor finish often suggests something about the quality of the merchandise. A cheap floor such as vinyl or carpet will wear out quickly and is often a quick fix, whilst an expensive floor such as granite or marble will have longevity and a sense of luxury.

There are many medium-cost flooring solutions that are durable and interesting in terms of pattern and colour, and work with the overall branded interior. Rubber, timber, ceramic or terrazzo tiles are favourable solutions.

The floor finish is used to define different areas within the store. Walkways, display areas and point of sale may all have different finishes within the same scheme.

Ceilings

The ceiling plays an important role in the feel of the entire retail space. It is the architectural element that sometimes goes unnoticed, but it is incredibly functional. Within the ceiling are light fittings, air-conditioning ducts, fire alarms, and sometimes sprinklers and music speakers. The general design principles for ceilings can be investigated through three different types: suspended ceilings, ceiling rafts and open ceilings.

The suspended ceiling is constructed from either a timber or metal frame suspended from the structural slab. This is then finished with a skin of material such as plasterboard. Proprietary systems are available and these will generally allow for access to the ceiling void for maintenance of equipment. The suspended ceiling leaves a void of 150–750 mm between the structural slab and the ceiling, providing enough room for all of the functions to be accommodated. This solution works very well in spaces that have a sufficient ceiling height to start with (so that the ceiling does not become too low) and gives a clean finish to the overall space.

Ceiling rafts are similar to a suspended ceiling in their construction, but will only cover areas of the ceiling space. They are often positioned over specific interior elements to create a design through the volume of the space, or to coincide with functional items hidden within the ceiling. Also, the material from which the raft is constructed may be quite adventurous and unique to the design scheme.

Figure 6.12 **BOLON EYEWEAR, Shanghai, Designer Pfarre Lighting Designer The use of a reflective ceiling creates the illusion of a larger space creating a room full of product. Here the walls and ceilings act in harmony with the tint of the mirror reinforcing the difference in planes.** © Shuhe Architectural Photography, Beijing via Pfarre Lighting Design

Figure 6.13
MALL OF SCANDINAVIA
Stockholm, **SWEDEN Designer, WINGÅRDHS, 2015**
This sculptural ceiling feature not only brings drama to the space but also aids navigation and legibility in a large space. The installation changes throughout the day using a mixture of natural and artificial light. © Johan Tägtström via Wingardhs

An open ceiling design is one where the ceiling structure is completely visible along with all of the servicing elements such as air conditioning, lighting and electrical services. If the store has a high ceiling then this design can appear industrial and may suit the requirements of the interior scheme. A common method of disguising the ceiling is to paint the ceiling and all of the fittings in black. This concept is taken from theatre design where blacked-out elements focus the viewer's eye on the entertainment. In retail, this masks the unsightly components and concentrates the shopper's view on the products. This is an effective solution that is often used in stores that have a lower budget – such as a retail outlet, which in most cases has a high ceiling. When the ceiling is low as can be found in existing older buildings or in basements, then the ceiling can be a challenge. A suspended ceiling cannot be used as there is not enough height, and the low ceiling means that nothing can be recessed within. In this instance, the best possible solution is to keep the ceiling as clear as possible, using the junction between the ceiling and walls to hide cables. Track lighting with wall-mounted fittings is the best option for lighting here.

These are the elements that make up the functional elements of the store's interior and contribute directly to the customers' experience in terms of how they interact with the product and brand. Increasingly display systems will have to accommodate more than product as they become part of the store narrative incorporating elements such as graphic images, interactive audio visual and archive elements.

The design of such fixtures sees the retail designer taking on a role very similar to that of a furniture designer, who in most cases is designing furniture or display fixtures for mass-production. Each fixture is designed down to the last detail, specifying all materials through to fixings. In some cases, off-the-shelf fixtures can be used or adapted to suit, and this may be an advantageous approach for small retailers, but for roll-out and premium retail, the bespoke piece can be cost-effective in terms of quantity or to convey an air of exclusivity with the use of high-quality materials.

> SARA MANUELLI
>
> 'British-crafted structures focus on the essence and techniques employed by Mulberry. . . bespoke leather mannequins, chandeliers and other ephemera aim to challenge the traditional division between shop-fitting and art.'

Figure 6.14 **MARNI STORE London, UK Designer, FUTURE SYSTEMS, 1999** Future Systems were invited to create a concept for all Marni stand-alone shops and units within department stores in London, Milan, Paris, New York, Tokyo and Kuwait. The store concept was generated by the textures, colour, composition and beauty of the clothes themselves, which were presented on sculptural islands, sitting against the brightly coloured backdrop of the shop.
© Future Systems via A_LA

In any retail fit-out, a contractor that is a specialist shopfitter will be employed to carry out all of the work on site. Also, in the case of a roll-out, the shopfitter will make the fixtures for every site to the drawings provided by the designer in the design manual. Using one contractor to make all of the fixtures usually cuts costs and maintains

quality, as they are then able to create tools to mass produce all of the internal fixtures.

The main elements of retail display consist of three basic elements: wall fixtures, mid-floor fixtures, and specialist elements that complete the functional aspect of the space.

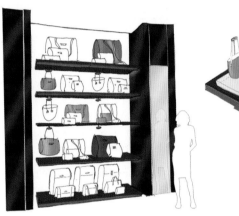

PERIMETER SHELF PRODUCT GROUPING
IMPLEMENTING ACRYLIC BLOCKS ONTO THE
SHELF FINISH ALLOWS PRODUCT TO BE
EMPHASISED AND MERCHANDISED IN
FAMILIES AND COLOUR RANGES

Figures 6.15 and 6.16 MULBERRY Concept store Designer, FOUR IV, 2008 These drawings show the development of an idea for wall fixtures for the Mulberry store concept. The walls are versatile and can take different formations of display. © Four IV

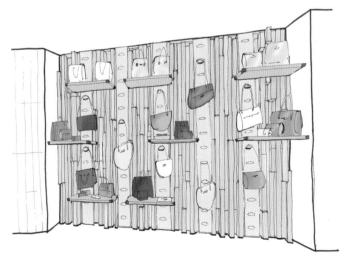

Wall fixtures

These are the principal unit for merchandise display and will generally consist of a series of bays of a standard module. The design of the wall fixture is created around standard size components to minimise joints whilst making the fixture more cost-effective and less time consuming to produce. These can be custom made by the shopfitters contracted to fit each site or bought as a standard kit. The most basic of panels is the slat wall, which is cheap and effective to use. This is a panel that has a series of evenly spaced tracks set within it from which to hang a standard set of hooks, shelves, brackets and rails. These can be bought in different finishes. There are other variations on the slat wall; some contain holes that take hooks, whilst others are planes with just a neutral finish.

A custom-made wall fixture can consist of a number of specialist design features that are unique to the store's scheme, but will always use the standard system of upright posts, hooks, brackets and rails.

When setting out the wall layout, each panel will have what is called a system upright post in between them. These posts have a series of slots that run down them and can hold shelf brackets and clothes rails. It is usual that the wall display will consist of a panel, a shelf at high level for product display and possibly a graphic, and then either a rail for hanging, more shelves evenly spaced, or hooks. It is also possible to connect cabinets to wall displays. These might be used for storage and can commonly be seen in mobile phone stores at the base of each bay; they could also be a glass cabinet for locking away valuable merchandise.

Some wall fixtures are more like pieces of grand furniture than a kit of parts. A men's clothing department displaying

Figure 6.17 **WALL FITMENTS, ADIDAS STORE** These form part of a simple language using painted steel uprights allowing the focus to be on the product. The flexibility allows for a variety of product stories and categories and also incorporates graphic panels and media. The same system has also been used in the mid floor fixtures to provide continuity. © Stephen Anderson

shirts and suits may be reminiscent of the design of a gentleman's club, for instance; and some appear to be built in, part of the architecture of the interior. In this case the designer is using the building to inform part of the design process, to mix in the architectural detail with the standard scheme, and it is seen more often in one-off stores or small roll-outs.

MARCEL WANDERS

'. . . product designers have a tendency to work more on details – to be innovative on the small parts and make things function.'

Figures 6.18 and 6.19 WHITE TOWER MUSEUM SHOP, Designer Kinnersley Kent Design, 2016 This wall unit has been specifically designed for the site and incorporates lighting as well as adjustable display elements. Great care has been taken with the materials used together with the craft-like nature of the elements and particularly the junction details; this reflects the quality of the products on display. © Kate Berry www.kateberry.co.uk

173

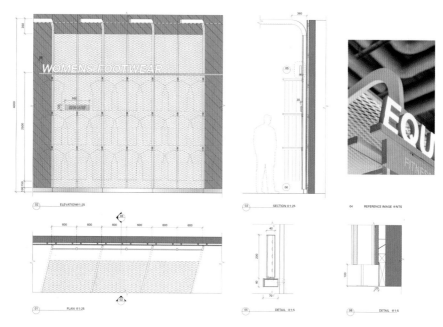

Figure 6.20 **WALL FIXTURE DETAIL,
Sports Corner, Qatar, Designer
Kinnersley Kent Design, 2014** This
example, for a leading sports retailer,
demonstrates how a wall fixture can be
customized using elements of standard
fixturing and materials. Notice how the
geometry is angled to help the customer
view the merchandise. © KKD

Mid-floor elements

There are many variations of mid-floor
elements that are used for a selection of
merchandising, display and interaction
activities.

These range from tables at different
heights and sizes, gondolas and
freestanding cabinets that hold
both storage and display through
to interactive areas which promote
customer engagement.

As well as an interesting display
feature, one of the important aspects
of the mid-floor fixture is to create
merchandising at different levels so that
the customer is drawn into the store to
view the displays beyond.

The table, often very simply
constructed, lends itself to low-
level display for smaller items and
accessories. Sometimes other
merchandising vehicles sit on the tables
to prop up merchandise effectively.
These are usually clear acrylic stands

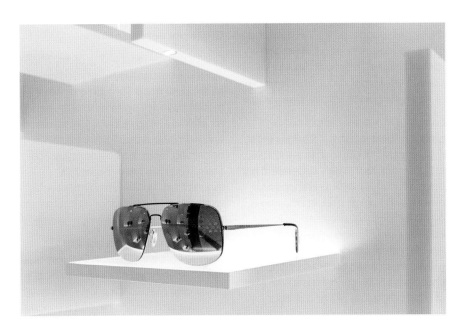

Figure 6.21 **BOLON, Shanghai, CHINA Designer Pfarre Lighting Design, 2016** This display detail is simple but effective using composite panels to create both the display shelf but also to house the concealed LED lighting above. © Shuhe Architectural Photography, Beijing via Pfarre Lighting Design

that are bought from specialist suppliers. Tables are sometimes stacked on top of each other to create more height.

The gondola is an element that works very hard. The design of a gondola can vary in terms of finishes, but almost all are constructed in the same way. It is most commonly used for clothing, but can also be adapted to hold shelves. It is usually designed and constructed using the same materials and fittings as the wall panels. This allows flexibility for the merchandise on display. The gondola is usually designed to be at eye-level height and will consist of a central panel, which sits on a rectangular frame with castors underneath. The panel could be solid or translucent, or simply be a frame, with system upright posts either side. A shelf sits close to the top of the unit for merchandise purposes and in most cases there will be a graphic panel above the shelf. The clothing rails or shelves are supported on brackets from the system upright posts. On both ends of the gondola are opportunities for further display. This would usually be used to tell a story about what is on the gondola such as an inspirational image.

From store to store, the cabinet is probably the item which changes most significantly in its size, shape and ability to hold stock as it is very dependent on the product. Mobile phone shops and other technological gadgets may be displayed on long, specially designed cabinets with storage underneath; jewellery stores favour timber cabinets with a glass case on top; and menswear shops tend to favour cabinets with slots or pigeon holes for ties and shirts.

Event and Interactive Elements

The display of product, however innovative and imaginative, is no longer the key imperative for people to visit a retail store. Increasingly they are looking to engage with the brand on a variety of levels; this might be to test, obtain information or simply to use the store as a social space. The design of the retail interior environment responds to this by creating exciting elements within the store. These are usually placed at specific areas within the layout, typically in the welcome space or as a focal point within the store.

The integration of media and technology to create an authentic engaging experience is increasingly important in the retail interior. This can range from a variety of sensory responses such as audio-visual through to tactile and engagement with product or activities.

Customer service points

One of the key focal points of any retail store is what used to be referred to as the cash desk. Through the use of mobile payment systems and the need for staff to engage more with customers and learn about their intentions this is becoming more of a customer service point. This may need to satisfy a range of functions from payment and wrapping through to offering customers loyalty cards and dealing with returns.

In its simplest form this element will need to house a till, which sometimes has a separate register and drawer, a credit card machine, a phone, a drawer for receipt rolls etc., a bin and a space to bag or pack merchandise. It is generally a solid object framed out of steel or timber, which is then clad in a variety of materials and finishes which will generally work with the overall scheme. The top is often staggered in height so that there is a separate area for staff equipment and a place at a comfortable height to write cheques or use a chip and pin. Also, the desk must have an area that is at a low level for wheelchair users.

The starting point for designing is an understanding of exactly what this equipment is, what its function is and the size of each component. Also, the products will demand certain functions from the point; in a clothing store for example, there needs to be space for discarding hangers and security tags whilst in in a supermarket there will need to be a conveyor belt.

Figure 6.22 NIKE FLAGSHIP STORE, NY, Nike Design 2016 This store demonstrates how the key elements enhance each other to create a great customer experience. The flooring creates flow and defines the individual areas. Within each category space there is a mixture of low mid-floor fixtures of both product and seating whilst higher wall units continue the product stories.

There are also numerous areas where customers interact such as the basketball court and an authentic running experience in which to try and test product. © Echochamber

Store layout

For this exercise you will need to think of a brand whose store you have never visited or that perhaps doesn't exist, for example this might be an 'online only' store.

Start by referring to the diagram on page 159, locating the main interior elements. Use this to begin to imagine how your brand might manifest itself in a physical store.

First draw out your own version of the diagram; don't worry too much about the shape as you can modify this later.

Begin to build up your drawing perhaps first using words but then enhancing this using sketches and images. Your aim is to try and create an idea of the interior using these principal elements.

You should consider the following:

What are your principal elements, surfaces and materials? You might want to refer to Chapter 4 here.

How is the space organized? What is the pace, how do people move through the space, particularly relative to the main display areas?

As you develop your ideas don't forget to add elements such as fitting rooms and perhaps toilets if required. Remember also to allow for storage and service areas.

Display elements

From the previous exercise you should now select one of your display elements which you will now look at in detail.

Decide what type of display element you wish to create and begin to draw what you want this to look like.

Consider the following:

Where will this be placed in the space?

How will it be fixed and what structure may be required?

What is the function of the display? This will help you develop the size and shape, if you are displaying clothing, for example, take measurements of the sort of clothes you wish to display.

Consider how people will use the displays and particularly the anthropometric data required, this will dictate the height of fittings and shelving.

Consider how you might want to light the merchandise you are displaying.

Figure 6.23 Burt's Bees, Hong Kong Designer: Landini Associates 2016 This dramatic feature, the honey wall, is made of replicated honey jars, each housing a different natural ingredient used by Burt's Bees in the manufacture of its products. The lighting is an important design feature– golden to recreate the magic of being inside a beehive, this encourages customers to dwell longer in-store, discovering Burt's Bees' story and range of products. © Landini Associates

We hope that you have enjoyed reading this book and found it both informative and thought provoking. The retail landscape is one of constant change and reinvention and with this book we hope to provide an overview of the basics at a particular point in time.

There will continue to be changes in shoppers' behaviour in the future and we have outlined a few key areas where this might take place over the following pages.

In the preceding chapters we have looked at the wider subject of retail and the drivers and design responses to this. In some respects we still view retail as a single activity; however, this is changing such that there is not one retail but multiple ways of brands engaging and forming relationships with their customers to exchange products, services and experiences. This will increasingly take place across an ever-widening range of channels and situations, at different times and in different modes. The key here will be to continue to maintain that sometimes fragile relationship between brands and their customers delivering the appropriate experience at each point.

The pace of change, largely driven by technology, is accelerating ever faster. The issues raised in Chapter 1 will become more extreme as consumers begin to test their new powers in the market place. The end of loyalty is being replaced by trust, largely in the ability to curate and customize choices for consumers in a world of widening choice; price, quality, must-have and utility. This is beginning to widen the framework of engagement encompassing lifestyle journalism, blogging, social media and sponsorship. Each of these will seek to persuade, influence and engage customers. The balance between online and store will continue to develop in a variety of formats with an increased melding of channels.

Ideas of experience in the retail environment will continue to develop in both macro and micro ways from entertainment and engagement through to simply having a knowledgeable chat with a sales associate. In Chapters 2 and 3 we have seen how the rise of the experience is a key driver for brands over a range of channels and formats. As we move towards omni channel retailing and beyond it will become increasingly important that each part of the brand experience delivers an appropriate response and memory. In many respects the retail environment is the human face of a brand and one of its key roles will be to allow staff to engage with customers as effectively as possible.

In the developed world of mass consumption we have a plethora of choices but increasingly we are looking for personal customized responses; this will be reflected in a variety of ways. One area in particular is the rise of the local store run either by an independent retailer or as part of a larger brand portfolio. Increasingly large format retailers are connecting with their customers through smaller curated outlets. This also allows them to expand their offer through options such as 'click and collect' and helps manage functions such as returns and product faults.

Some years ago Stephen made a presentation at a retail conference about the value of the small local shop. There were a few raised eyebrows from the professionals present who regarded him as slightly eccentric. However, communities are now beginning to value the importance of small local stores which cater for their individual needs and recognize them with a welcoming smile. This change is in response to changing habits, particularly in terms of convenience grocery shopping where consumers are increasingly shopping for fewer items with greater frequency.

The relationship that brands have with their customers will become even closer. This relationship will be leveraged through knowledge of existing purchasing and intentions through to online and in-store behaviour. Retailers are using this to create what is termed 'price fluidity' which can take a number of forms but in its most basic form is the customization of price to a particular customer. Examples range from higher prices for those living in more affluent areas through to discount deals for

: **FITCH: RETAIL AND BRAND CONSULTANCY, FX MAGAZINE 2016**

'By providing multiple services in one location, stores will place themselves at the heart of the community.'

customer loyalty. We have looked at the area of beacon technology in stores, but brands are now looking at customers' online profiles such as Facebook to determine their preferences and potential purchasing decisions. It is possible that in the future some customers may begin to feel uncomfortable with these intrusions and brands will need to respond to this with sensitivity. In other areas, to maintain their cachet, high-end brands are limiting their online sales of products to registered partners to deter discounting.

It has been interesting that many of the consultancies that we engaged with in writing this book were reticent to predict any overall vision of a retail environment of the future and for good reason. We are not in the business of prediction but one thing that we will caution against is the idea of a linear path to the future and the idea of 'because we can we will'. There have been many prophetic predictions regarding the role of technology, if we were to believe the predictions of the 1950s and 60s we would be eating protein pills rather than meals when in fact quite the opposite has happened. We have become more interested in what we eat and how our food is prepared, largely as a response to a range of food scares. The idea of online shopping as a golden age may be waning as our streets become increasingly clogged with vans delivering and returning product with driverless vehicles offering no panacea.

We have heard many times about the death of the retail store but to slightly misquote Mark Twain, these may have been greatly exaggerated.

Adcock, P. Supermarket Shoppology: The Science of Supermarket Shopping: And a Strategy to Spend Less and Get More, Woodstock: Writersworld, 2014

Anderson, J. & Shiers, D. The Green Guide to Specification: Breeam Specification, Wiley Blackwell; 4th Edition, 2009

Beylerian, G. & Dent, A. Material Connexion: The Global Resource for Innovative Materials for Artists, Architects and Designers, Thames & Hudson, 2005

Brooker, G. & Stone, S. Rereadings: Interior Architecture and the Design Principles of Remodelling Existing Buildings, RIBA Enterprises, 2004

Brown, R. & Farrelly, L. Materials and Interior Design, Laurence King 2012

de Chatel, F. & Hunt, R. Retailisation: The Here, There and Everywhere of Retail, Europa Publications, 2003

Coleman, P. Shopping Environments: Evolution, Planning and Design, RIBA Press 2006

Conran, T. A Sort of Autobiography Q&A, Harper Collins, 2001

Curtis, E. Fashion Retail Wiley-Academy, 2004

Dean, C. The Inspired Retail Space, Rockport Publishers, 2003

Din, R. New Retail, Conran Octopus, 2000

Fitch, R. Fitch on Retail Design, Phaidon Press Limited, 1990

Fogg, M. Boutique: A 60s Cultural Phenomenon, Mitchell Beazley, 2003

Giest, J. F. Arcades: The History of a Building Type, MIT Press, 1983

Green, W. The Retail Store Design and Construction, iUniverse.com, 1991

Gridley, N. & Kusume, Y. Brand Romance: Using the Power of High Design to Build a Lifelong Relationship with Your Audience, Palgrave Macmillan, 2013

Higgins, I. Spatial Strategies for Interior Design, Laurence King, 2015

Klein, N. No Logo Flamingo, 2000

Lancaster, B. The Department Store: A Social History, Leicester University Press, 1995

Major, M. & Spears, J. Made of Light, The Art of Light and Architecture, Birkhäuser, 2005

Manuelli, S. Design for Shopping: New Retail Interiors, Laurence King Publishing, 2006

Massey, A. Interior Design Since 1900, Thames and Hudson, 2008

McDonough, W. & Braungart, M. Cradle to Cradle: Remaking the Way We Make Things, Rodale Press, 2003

Miller, M. B. The Bon Marché: Bourgeois Culture and the Department Store, 1869–1920 George Allen & Unwin, 1981

Moreno, S. et al. Forefront: The Culture of Shop Window Design, Birkhäuser, 2005

Moxon, S. Sustainability in Interior Design, Laurence King, 2012

Mun, D. Shops: A Manual of Planning and Design, The Architectural Press,1981

Neumeier, M. The Brand Gap, Pearson Education, 2003

Olins, W. The Brand Handbook Thames & Hudson, 2008

Pallasmaa, J. The Eyes of the Skin: Architecture and the Sense, John Wiley & Sons, 2008

Pegler, M. Designing the Brand Identity in Retail Spaces, Bloomsbury, 2015

Plunkett, D. & Reid, O. Detail in Contemporary Retail Design, Laurence King, 2012

Ries, A. & Ries, L. The 22 Immutable Laws of Branding, Harper Collins, 1998

Riewoldt, O. Brandscaping: Worlds of Experience in Retail Design, Birkhauser Publishers, 2002

Scott, K. Shopping Centre Design, Von Nostrand Reinhold Co. Ltd, 1989

Steel, C. Hungry City: How Food Shapes Our Lives, Chatto & Windus, 2008

Thorne, R. Covent Garden Market: Its History and Restoration, The Architectural Press, 2008

Turner, A. W. The Biba Experience, Roger Sears and Isobel Gilan, 2004

Vernet, D. & de Wit, L. Boutiques and Other Retail Spaces: The Architecture of Seduction, Routledge, 2007

Yelavich, S. Contemporary World Interiors, Phaidon, 2007

Zumthor, P. Atmospheres Birkhäuser, 2006

Webology

BREEAM (https://www.breeam.org)

A Continuous Lean (https://www.acontinuous lean.com)

The Cool Hunter (https://www.thecoolhunter .co.uk)

Coresight Research (https://www.fungglobal retailtech.com)

designboom (https://www.designboom.com)

Design Council UK (https://www.designcouncil .org.uk)

Dezeen (https://www.dezeen.com)

Echo Chamber (https://echochamber.com)

Material District (https://materialdistrict.com)

Monocle (https://monocle.com)

Quote sources

Chapter 1

Oxford English Dictionary, https://en.oxford dictionaries.com/definition/retail accessed May 2016

Millennials Myths & Realities, CBRE Report, 2016

Interview with David Dalziel, Creative Director, Dalziel & Pow, 2016

Bennet R. Engaging Brands: Brands Behaving Differently, Dalziel & Pow, accessed from website http://www.dalziel-pow.com/opinion /engaging-brands-brands-behaving-differently / November 2016

Anne Pitcher, Managing Director, Selfridges taken from Arlidge J. Are you being served?, Sunday Times Magazine, 2016

Holt D. Quelch J. &Taylor E. How Global Brands Compete, Harvard Business Review, 2004

Anderson C. The Long Tail, Hyperion, 2006

Armstrong S. The Future of Retail, 2016

Kramers L. Brand Director, Kinnersley Kent Design in Generation Game, FX Magazine, March 2017

Chapter 2

The Power of Branding, Design Council, accessed from https://www.designcouncil.org .uk/news-opinion/power-branding, July 2016

Knight, P. Nike, taken from De Chatel, F. and Hunt, R. Retailisation: The Here, There and Everywhere of Retail, Europa Publications, 2003

Interview with Paul Nicholson, Director, Chalk Architecture, 2016

Olins, W. The Brand Handbook, Thames & Hudson, 2008

From Hunter Press Release, 2018

Reitwoldt, O. Brandscaping: Worlds of Experience in Retail Design, Birkhäuser, 2002

Din, R. New Retail Conran Octopus, 2000

Grefe R. What can designers do to improve their prospects? From https://www.aiga.org /what-can-designers-do-to-improve-their -prospects, 2010

Olins, W. The Wolff Olins Guide to Corporate Identity, Design Council, 1990

Neumeier M. The Brand Gap, Pearson Education, 2003

Koolhaas, R. taken from De Chatel, F. and Hunt, R. Retailisation: The Here, There and Everywhere of Retail, Europa Publications, 2003

Interview with David Dalziel, Creative Director, Dalziel & Pow, 2016

Chapter 3

Gardner, J. in The New York Sun. Taken from www.bcj.com August 2009

JWT Research, New trend report: Frontier(less) Retail, https://www.jwtintelligence.com/2016 /06/new-trend-report-frontierless-retail/, 2016

Wade R. Boxpark CEO taken from Rpberts M. Opinion: Invested in Human Experience Retail Focus http://www.retail-focus.co.uk/features /3295-opinion-invested-in-human-experience January 2018

Conran, T. A Sort of Autobiography Q&A, HarperCollins, 2001

Howard S. Head of Sustainability taken from Farrell S. We've Hit Peak Home Furnishings, Says Ikea Boss, The Guardian, 2016

Deep Dive: The Mall Is Not Dead: Part 1, Fung Global Retail & Technology Report 2016

Scott, K Shopping Centre Design, Von Nostrand Reinhold Co. Ltd, 1989

Paula Nickolds: CEO John Lewis taken from Arlidge J. Are You Being Served?, Sunday Times Magazine, 2016

Din, R. New Retail, Conran Octopus, 2000

Chapter 4

Pallasmaa, J. The Eyes of the Skin: Architecture and the Sense, John Wiley & Sons, 2008

Heap, D. from www.danheap.com/about.html August 2009

Zumthor, P. Atmospheres, Birkhäuser, 2006

Chapter 5

Underhill P. Why We Buy, The Science of Shopping, Orion Business, 1999

Green, W. The Retail Store Design and Construction, iUniverse.com, 1991

Saguez & Partners, Lafayette Maison Press Release, 2004

Chapter 6

Moreno S. et al. Forefront: The Culture of Shop Window Design, Birkhäuser, 2005

Brooker, G. & Stone, S. Rereadings: Interior Architecture and the Design Principles of Remodelling Existing Buildings, RIBA Enterprises, 2004

Manuelli, S. Design for Shopping: New Retail Interiors, Laurence King Publishing, 2006

Wanders, M. taken from Manuelli, S. Design for Shopping: New Retail Interiors, Laurence King Publishing, 2006

Acoustics The word acoustic describes the scientific study of sound. In terms of the interior, sound can be controlled through the use of materials. Hard materials will bounce sound around a space, creating echoes, whilst soft materials will absorb sound, providing a quieter space.

Arcade An enclosed public shopping area with impressive glass and steel roof structures and ornate decorative facades, which often creates a passageway between high streets.

Atrium A covered interior space with a glass domed roof, often found in arcades and in the central circulation space of a department store.

Boutique A small independent fashion retailer, often with a distinct fashion style.

Branding Branding is an approach to marketing products and services under a particular name that has an appeal to a focused group of people. A brand can be a product, a person or a logo. Anything that can be bought and sold as an idea or artefact can be branded.

Brandscaping This is a term used to describe the mapping of a brand into a three-dimensional space.

Chain store The chain store is a design scheme for a retailer that is repeated from city to city.

Channel A conduit for delivering goods and services.

Circulation A controlled route one takes around a building.

Concept store A concept store is a retail space that is used to test and promote new retail formats for the first time, in a specific location.

Concessions Concessions are spaces occupied within a department store by key retailers or labels. Concessions are grouped together on each floor depending on the product.

Concourse The volume of space before or between platforms at train stations and airports.

Consumerism The purchase of products, services or experiences.

'Cradle to cradle' This is a term used to describe the constant cyclical reuse of materials: the material is born, used, removed and reused.

Department store A large purpose-built building for retail that houses a range of products and labels in the form of concessions.

Façade The façade is the front elevation of a building. In retailing, the façade acts as an advertisement for the store within, displaying signage and large plate glass windows for display purposes.

Fail Point A stage in the experience when the reality does not deliver the brand promise, sometimes referred to as Pain Point.

Fashion house A premium fashion label, which has a collection of designers or one key designer working under its name.

Fixture The term used to describe specially designed pieces of furniture that hold product and display merchandise.

Flagship store is an idealized retail experience, where a retailer will promote the brand in large prominently positioned sites around the world. It is usually fitted out to a high specification and with unique features that act as a brand statement; there is likely to be a high level of experience and interpretation. The idea is to stimulate desire for the brand's products across a wide range of channels.

Gondola A type of fixture that holds hanging garments in a mid-floor position and is usually head height.

Hypermarket A hypermarket is a larger version of a supermarket and will often house a generous variety of products that go beyond grocery shopping.

Lifestyle store A lifestyle store encapsulates a range of products under one venue or brand name, giving the consumer the opportunity to buy into a whole lifestyle experience at a single point.

Lux The way in which the brightness of light is measured.

Mega centre A large out-of-town retail experience that usually combines retail with leisure facilities.

Mood boards A mood board consists of a series of precedent images arranged on a board to describe the feel of the interior space and the nature of the user.

Omnichannel The seamless combination of in-store and online experiences across a range of platforms and channels. This may range from social and mobile media to personal interaction to in-store events.

Pace Pace describes the speed at which someone moves around the store. Retail designers often consider a range of paces within an interior scheme.

Pop-up store A pop-up store is a temporary retail environment that is set up to promote the brand in unusual places, often with an exclusive range of products that are not available in-store or sometimes purely as an interactive advertisement without product.

Product An object or artefact.

Retail unit A custom-built space for retail purposes.

Roll-out A term used to describe the reproduction of an interior scheme into a number of different locations. Although the scheme may need to be altered to reflect the nature of the site, the principles behind the design idea remain the same.

Shadow gap A contemporary detail used to create a junction between a wall and a ceiling or floor; or between a fixture and the floor that makes the objects displayed on it appear to be floating.

Sustainability Using the Earth's natural resources through energy consumption, building and making materials in a way that does not impact on the environment.

System upright posts Thin, steel posts with a series of slots running up the front face that are used between wall panels to hold rails and shelf brackets.

Virtual shopping A non-physical retail space accessible online.

Image Credits